The Mammoth Dictionary of 960 Pages
Sumerian-English Dictionary: Vocabulary And History
Part II

Comparative Lexicon of Sumerian, Akkadian, Assyrian, Babylonian, Chaldean, Phoenician, Ugaritic, Hittite, Aramaic, Syriac, Hebrew, Arabic.
First Edition
Available in paperback at www.lulu.com

Maximillien de Lafayette

This dictionary is available in 2 formats:
1-Amazon Kindle edition at www.amazon.com
2-In paperback at www.lulu.com

TIMES SQUARE PRESS

New York   Berlin   Paris

2013

2013

Printed by Times Square Press.
Date of Publication: January 27, 2013.

Maximillien de Lafayette's books are available in 2 formats:
1-Amazon Kindle edition at www.amazon.com
2-In paperback at www.lulu.com

Author's website:

Note on Pronunciation

- a...Like in Matthew.
- Á...Light but prolonged accent.
- À...Grave accent.
- š....Like in sash. Put a heavy accent on the sh.
- i....Like in kiwi.
- u...Like in full.
- h...Like in Jose, in Spanish. Put a heavy accent on the J.
- ñ...Like España in Spanish. It sounds like n'ya.; Espa'n'ya.

For Akkadian and Chaldean words:
- H replaces the character ḫ
- sz or c replace the character š which is pronounced as sheh
- s replaces the character ṣ
- t replaces the character ṭ , which is pronounced teth
- ' (Apostrophe) replaces the character aleph ʾ
- y is used instead of j

For Hittite words:
- ē is pronounced like eeh

For Arabic and Hebrew words:
'H, pronounced like 'het, and sometimes like Kha.
ch (chaf) is pronounced like "ch", or "Kaf."
u is pronounced like oo.
ah is pronounced like a.
'a is pronounced like ah.
Q (quf) is pronounced like kaf.

5

A Sumerian cosmetics container.

A Sumerian vessel.

A Sumerian drinking vessel, circa 2,550-2,450 B.C.

gišTigidlu: Noun. A musical instrument, possibly a flute or a piccolo.

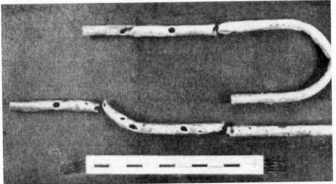

A Sumerian flute.

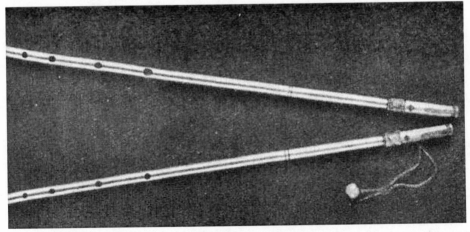

Silver double-flute from Ur.

gišTir: Noun.
a-A wood,
b-A forest,
c-A wooden area.

gišTukul: Noun.
a-A weapon,
b-A mace.

lúTúg-du8: Noun.
a- A woven cloth maker,
b-A felt maker,
c-Cloth craftsman,
d-Cloth artisan,
e-A weaver,
f-A tailor,
g-A dressmaker.

*** *** ***

U

Ù: Adjective.
a-High,
b-Elevated,
c-High ground,
d-A powerful person,
e-Physically strong.

Ú: Noun. A plant.

Ú: Noun.
a-A man of power,
b-An influential person,
c-Food,
d-Plant,
e-Green grass,
f-Vegetables.

Ú: Preposition.
a-If,
b-After,
c-When.

Ú: Verb:
a-To nourish,
b-To support,
c-To stand by.

U11-ri2-in: Noun.
a-An eagle,
b-A vulture.

13

U$_3$: Noun.
a-A scream,
b-An argument,
c-A dispute,
d-Yelling,
e-A duel,
f-A fight.

U$_3$: Verb.
a-To lean over,
b-To bend over,

U$_4$: Noun.
a-A scream,
b-An argument,
c-A dispute,
d-Yelling,
e-A duel.

U$_4$: Noun.
a-The day,
b-The time,
c-A period.

U$_4$-a: Preposition. Adverb.
a-When it happened,
b-At the time,
c-When,
d-At that moment,
e-Passage of time,
f-A period of time.

U$_4$-a-gin$_7$: Adverb.Preposition.
a-During,
b-When,
c-While,
d-At the time.

U$_4$-a-ta: Adverb.
a-After,
b-Later on,
c-Following.

U$_4$-ba: Adverb. Preposition.
a-Previously,
b-Before,
c-Formerly,
d-At that time,
e-During that time,
f-While.

U$_4$-bar$_7$: Noun. Adverb. Midday.

U$_4$-bita: Adverb. Preposition.
a-From the moment,
b-Since,
c-From the early time,
d-Hence,
e-Thus.

U$_4$-bi-ta: Noun.
a-The past,
b-Yesteryears.

U$_4$d: Noun.
a-A day,
b-Time,
c-A period.

U$_4$-da: Noun.
a-Today,
b-At the present time.

U$_4$-da: Preposition. Adverb.
a-When,

15

b-While,
c-Whenever,
d-If,
e-In case,
f-During.

U$_4$-è: Noun. The sunrise.

U$_4$-šú: Noun. The sunset.

U$_4$-sud-ra: Adverb.
a-Forever,
b-Permanently,
c-Perpetually,
d-Constantly.

U$_4$-šú-uš: Adverb.
a-Every day,
b-Daily,
c-On a daily basis,
d-Day by day.

U$_4$-te-en: Noun. The evening.

U$_4$-te-na: Noun. The morning.

U$_4$-ul-la; u$_4$-ì-li: Noun.
a-The next day,
b-The following day,
c-The day after,
d-Tomorrow.

U$_5$: Adjective.
a-Elevated,
b-High,
c-Upper ground,
d-Raised up,
e-Way up.

U$_5$: Adverb.
a-Totally (Totality),
b-All of it,
c-Entirely (In its entirety),
d-Everything.

U$_5$: Noun.
a-A hut,
b-A tent,
c-A shelter,
d-Elevated land,
e-Upper area,
f-A small hill,
g-A bird,
h-A cock,
i-Totality.

U$_5$: Verb.
a-To travel,
b-To ride,
c-To sail,
d-To conduct,
e-To lead,
f-To guide.

U$_5$-bímušen: Noun.
a-A bird,
b-A wild goose.

U$_6$ -du$_{11}$: Verb.
a-To inspire,
b-To influence,
c-To admire,
d-To wonder,
e-To incite,
f-To cause,
g-To provoke,
h-To revere,

17

U$_6$-di: Noun.
a-Admiration,
b-Amazement,
c-Astonishment,

U$_6$-ga: Adjective,
a-Inspiring,
b-Inspirational,
c-Influential,
d-Splendid,
e-Fabulous,
f-Striking.

U$_6$-nir: Noun.
a-A Ziggurat structure,
b-A Ziggurat complex,
c-Temple's blueprints.

U$_8$: Noun.
a-A scream,
b-An argument,
c-A dispute,
d-Yelling,
e-A duel.

U$_8$: Verb.
a-To support,
b-To retain,
c-To reinforce,
d-To lift,
e-To carry.

Ú-a: Adjective.
a-An assistant,
b-A helper,
c-An aide,
d-A care-giver.
e-A care-taker.

18

Ub: Noun.
a-A place,
b-A position,
c-A nest,
d-An angle,
e-A sanctuary,
f-An altar,
g-A small room.

Úb: Noun.
a-A venom,
b-A malice,
c-A vicious intention.

Ub$_3$: Noun:
a-A flea,
b-A moth,
c-An insect,
d-Lice,
e-A poison,
f-An insect bite.

Ub$_4$: Noun.
a-A ditch,
b-A trench,
c-A hole,
d-An excavation.

Ubara: Noun.
a-A support,
b-A sponsorship,
c-A shield,
d-A protection.

Ubšu-ukkinna: Noun.
a-A gathering,
b-A reunion,

c-A meeting,
d-A council,
e-An assembly.

Ùbu-bul: Noun.
a-A spark,
b-A flame,
c-A fire.

Ud: Adjective.
a-Bright,
b-Sunny.

Ud: Noun. A day.

Ud: Noun.
a-The sun,
b-The weather,
c-The storm.

Ud: Preposition.
a-Since,
b-When.

Udu: Noun.
a-Sheep,
b-A goat,
c-A ram.

Ú-du$_{11}$-g: Noun.
a-Entities,
b-Spirits,
c-Djinns,
d-Demons.

Udug: Noun.
a-A demon,
b-A bad spirit,

c-A malevolent entity,
d-A demonic creature.

A kneeling subject being attacked by demonic creatures, circa 2000-1600 B.C. Isin-Larsa.

Údug: Noun. A weapon.

Udun: Noun.
a-A stove,
b-A furnace,

c-An oven.

Udun-mah: Noun.
a-A community cooking oven, usually used by villagers (Women bakers) in a place located around the main plaza of the village. The oven is made from baked clay, and fired bricks.
b-A public stove.
c-A baking furnace.

Ùĝ : Noun.
a-A group of people,
b-A gathering,
c-An assembly,
d-A meeting,
e-A reunion,
f-A small crowd.

Ug: Noun. A lion.

Ug: Noun.
a-Anger,
b-Fury,
c-Hate,
d-A lion.

Ug: Verb.
a-To destroy,
b-To kill,
c-To die,
d-To perish,
e-To annihilate.

Ug$_4$: Noun. Death.

Ug$_5$: Noun. Adjective. A dead person.

Ug$_5$: Verb.
a-To die,

b-To perish.

Ug$_6$: Adjective.
a-Amazed,
b-Astonished,
c-Amazing,
d-Astonishing,
e-Impressed,
f-Impressive.

Ug$_6$: Noun.
a-Astonishment,
b-Admiration,
c-Amazement,
d-Perplexity.

Ug$_6$: Verb.
A-To gaze at,
b-To observe,
c-To watch,
d-To stare at.

Ug$_7$: Verb.
a-To perish,
b-To die.

Ug$_7$: Noun.
a-Animal corpses,
b-Dead animals.

Ug$_7$: Noun.
a-Death,
a-A dead person.

Ug$_8$: Noun. Death.

Ùĝdaga: Noun.
a-Neighbors.

b-People living nearby.

Ùĝ-íl: Noun.
a-A holder,
b-A messenger,
c-A bearer.

Uĝnim: Noun.
a-A military troop,
b-An army,
c-A crowd,
d-A military maneuver,
e-A training camp.

Ugu: Noun.
a-The head,
b-The forehead,
c-Top of the head,
d-A skull.

Ugu: Preposition.
A-Upon,
b-Later,
c-Over.

Ugu: Pronoun.
a-Him,
b-Her,
c-That,
d-This one,
e-This,
f-Them.

Úgu: Verb.
a-To run away,
b-To escape,
c-To evade,
d-To disappear,

e-To vanish,
f-To hide,
g-To retreat,
h-To flee.

Ù-gul: Noun.
a-Begging,
b-A plea,
c-An appeal.

Ugula: Noun.
a-A supervisor,
b-A controller,
c-An inspector,
d-A person in charge,
e-A foreman,
f-A captain,
g-A commanding officer.

Ù-gulĝar: Verb.
a-To beg,
b-To request with humility,
c-To appeal to.

Úgun: Noun.
a-A lady,
b-A mistress,
c-A lover,
d-A paramour,
e-A concubine,
f-A confidant.

Úgur-igi: Noun. The eyebrow.

Úhluh: Noun. A cough.

Ukken: Noun.
a-An assembly,

b-A meeting.

Ukkin: Noun.
a-An assembly,
b-A meeting.

Ùku: Noun.
a-A gathering,
b-A group of people,
c-Masses,
d-A crowd,
e-An assembly,
f-A council,
g-A meeting.

Ùku$_4$: Verb. To fall asleep.

Uku$_5$: Noun. Poverty.

Ukum: Noun. The dust

Úkur: Noun. A butcher.

Ukur$_3$: Noun. A pauper.

Ukur$_4$: Noun. A pauper.

Ul: Adjective.
a-Beautiful,
b-Plesant.

Ul: Noun.
a-Happiness,
b-Delight,
c-Joy
d-Excitement,
e-Satisfaction,
f-Pleasure,

g-Beauty,
h-A flower,
i-A rose.

Ul$_4$: Verb.
a-To move fast,
b-To hurry up,
c-To act quickly,
d-To put pressure on a person,
e-To intimidate,
f-To annoy,
g-To harass.

Ul$_4$-la-bé: Adverb.
a-Promptly,
b-Right away,
c-Quickly,
d-Suddenly.

Ul-a: Adverb.
a-Happily,
b-Joyfully,
c-With excitement.

Úlá: Verb.
a-To decrease,
b-To limit,
c-To reduce,
d-To resize,
e-To diminish.

Ula$_5$: Verb.
a-To enjoy,
b-To rejoice.

Úli: Noun.
a-Plants,
b-Herbs,

c-Vegetation,
d-Spices.

Ull: Adjective.
a-Bright,
b-Far away,
c-Ancient,
d-Archaic,
e-Primitive,
f-Back in time,
g-Old,
h-Lasting,
i-Distant,
j-Remote,
k-Out of reach,
l-Beyond reach,
m-Unattainable.

Ull: Noun.
a-A wild flower,
b-A rose,
c-A decoration,
d-A star.

Ull: Verb.
a-To shine,
b-To glitter.

Ul-lía: Adjective.
a-Archaic,
b-Very old,
c-Ancient.

Ulšárra: Noun.
a-A joy,
b-An enchantment
c-A delight,
d-A jubilation.

U-Lu: Conjunction.
A-Or,
b-Either.

Ùlu: Noun. The south wind.

Ù-luh: Noun. A scepter.

Ù-luh-ha- sù: Noun.
a-Branches,
b-Leaves.

Ulul$_2$: Noun.
a-A rope,
b-A chain,
c-A thread,
d-A leach.

Úlutin: Adjective.
a-Attractive,
b-Appealing.

Um: Noun.
a-A mother,
b-A care-giver,
c-An old woman.

Ù-ma: Noun.
a-A victory,
b-A triumph,
c-A big success.

Úma-am: Noun. Animals.

Umah: Noun.
a-A swamp,
b-A marsh,
c-Stagnant water.

A Sumerian swamp.

An Iraqi marsh with reed houses, the Sumerian old-fashion way.

A Sumerian reed house in a swamp/marsh area of Mesopotamia.

Iraqi marshes.

Iraqi marshes with reed and mud houses, quite similar to the
ancient Sumerian homes, built thousands of years ago.

Umbin: Noun.
a-A nail,
b-A claw.

Ummi-a: Noun.
a-A scribe,

Statue of a Sumerian scribe, circa 2,500 B.C.

34

Sumerian scribes.

b-A teacher,
c-A writer,
d-A scholar.

Sumerian/Mesopotamian scribes, who also served as teachers
and scholars.

Ùmmu: Noun.
a-A water container,
b-A water bag made from animal skin.

Umu: Noun.
a-A tutor,
b-A teacher,
c-A guide,
d-An instructor,
e-A mentor.

Umum: Noun.
a-Wisdom,

b-Experience,
c-Knowledge,
d-Learning,
e-Scholarship,
f-A master,
g-A lord,
h-A man of a great authority.

Ùmun: Noun.
a-A flea,
b-An insect.

Úmun: Noun.
a-Wisdom,
b-Experience,
c-Knowledge,
d-Learning,
e-Scholarship,
f-Know-how.

Umun$_{11}$: Noun.
a-A Marsh,
b-A stagnant water,
b-A swamp,
d-A pond,
e-A pool.

Umun$_5$: Noun.
a-Stagnant water,
b-A swamp,
d-A pond.

Umun$_{11}$: Noun.
a-Stagnant water,
b-A swamp,
d-A pond,
e-A pool,
f-A marsh.

Umuš: Noun.
a-A good judgment,
b-A wise decision,
c-Consideration,
d-A common sense.

Ùñ: Noun.
a-A gathering,
b-A group of people,
c-Masses,
d-A crowd.

Ùña: Noun.
a-A gathering,
b-A group of people,
c-Masses,
d-A crowd.

Ù-na: Noun.
a-A victory,
b-A triumph,
c-A big success.

Unken: Noun.
a-An assembly,
b-A meeting,
c-A reunion,
d-A council.

Unu₂: Noun.
a-A fortress,
b-A castle,
c-A dwelling,
d-A settlement,
e-A habitat,
f-A citadel.

A Sumero-Assyrian citadel.

Stone carved staircase leading to the entrance of a citadel.

A Babylonian-Sumerian citadel.

Unu₆: Noun.
a-An elevated shrine,
b-A temple,
c-A sanctuary.

A Sumerian seal depicting a leader in front of a temple's façade.

Unug₂: Noun.
a-A habitat,
b-A settlement,
c-A fort,
d-A dwelling.

Ùnug: Noun.
a-An elevated shrine,
b-A temple,
c-A sanctuary.

Úp: Adjective.
a-A vicious intention,
b-A malicious deed.

Úp: Noun.
a-A venom,
b-A poison,
c-A malice.

Ur: Adjective.
a-Modest,
b-Humble.

Ur: Noun.
a-A servant,
b-A warrior,
c-A soldier,
d-An infantry-soldier,
e-An archer,
f-A young man,
g-A foe,
h-A rival,
i-A competitor,
j-A dog.

Ùr: Noun.
a-An arch,
b-A foyer,
c-An entrance,
d-An elevation,
e-A small hill,
f-A roof,
g-Wood logs to support a flat roof,
 h-Tree logs used to support the upper part of a bridge,
i-Organs,
j-Humam body parts,
k-The base,
l-A foundation perimeter,

m-A construction site.

A spear-man from Ur.

An archer from Mari.

An infantry-soldier from Lagash.

A soldier as a royal guard.

Ur, the city of: Noun. Old Babylonian/Sumerian/Akkadian.
One of the earliest settlements of the Anunnaki in the Middle
East. It was at Ur, that Abraham learned about the Anunnaki
gods, Enlil, Ea, Enki, and developed his idea of one god
governing the entire universe.

Ur

Ruins of the city of Ur in Iraq.

Ur is located near the town of Nasiriya, about 365 km south of
Baghdad, Iraq.
Ur was the hometown of Patriarch Abraham, where he had
several encounters with the Anunnaki Lords and Sinhars.
It was at Ur, that Abraham was introduced to Enki and Enlil, and
received his first esoteric guidance.

Above and below: Ruins of Ur.

Panel One: Days of assaults and war.

Two scenes (Panel One and Panel Two) from the life in Ur (The Royal Standards of Ur, circa 2,600-2,400 B.C.)

Panel Two: Days of prosperity and peace.

In panel one, the king depicted in the center leads his soldiers and chariots to war. In panel two, we see the prosperity days of Ur. In the top row, third from left, the king of Ur is a peaceful man; he is celebrating his military triumph, and enjoying music, while drinking with his subjects. In the lower rows, we see his subjects bringing gifts and offerings.

Ur: Verb.
a-To tremble,
b-To shake,
c-To delete,
d-To smear,
e-To wipe out,
f-To remove,
g-To encircle,
h-To limit.

Ur$_{11}$-ru: Verb.
a-To work the field,
b-To prepare the soil,
c-To cultivate,
d-To farm,
e-To till.

Ur$_2$: Verb.
a-To tremble,
b-To encircle,
c-To surround,
d-To delete,
e-To remove.

Ur$_3$: Verb.
a-To remove,
b-To encircle,
c-To limit,
d-To wipe out.

Ur$_4$: Verb.
a-To limit,
b-To surround,
c-To retain inside,
d-To remove,
e-To push aside.

Ur$_4$-ur$_4$: Verb.

47

a-To ruin,
b-To decimate.

Ur$_5$-bi: Adverb.
a-Together,
b-Nearby.

Ur$_5$-tud: Noun.
a-A maid,
b-A servant.

Ur$_5$-tuku: Noun.
a-A loan officer,
b-A debtor,
c-A creditor.

Ur$_7$: Noun. Father-in-law.

Urbar-ra: Noun. A wolf.

Ur-bé-gu$_7$: Verb.
a-To fight in a group or in a pack,
b-To confront,
c-To press,
d-To assault,
e-To clash.

Urbi: Adverb.
a-Together,
b-Nearby.

Urd: Noun.
a-Lands,
b-Territory,
c-Kingdom.

Úrgu: Noun.
a-Ferocity,

b-Fury,
c-Rage,
d-Brutality.

Uri$_2$: Noun.
a-A doorpost,
b-A gate-post.

Uri$_5$ki-m: Noun. Name of the city of Ur.

Úriki-m: Noun. Name of the city of Ur.

Urim$_2$: Noun. A doorpost.

Urim$_5$: Noun. A doorpost.

Ùri-n: Noun.
a- A gate-post,
b-A doorpost,
c-A gate-pole.

Urin: Noun.
a-A sign,
b-A display,
c-A flag,
d-A protocol,
e-A logo,
f-A banner,
g-A symbol.

Ùrin: Noun.
a-An eagle,
b-A vulture,
c-Blood.

Ùri-n: Noun. Adjective.
a-Blood,
b-Bloody.

Urmah: Noun. A lion.

Ur-Nammu, King: Noun. Sumerian/Akkadian/Babylonian.
(Third Dynasty of Ur (2044 to 2007 B.C.) Ur-Nammu's empire
lasted about 105 years.
According to Babylonian legends and inscriptions, Ur-Nammu
received orders from his god and goddess to build the ziggurat,
interpreted by some Biblical scholars as the Tower of Babel.
This story was recorded on a stele known to historians and
archeologists as "A tower unto the heavens."
King Ur-Nammu rebuilt and enlarged one of the most important
temples in ancient Mesopotamia - the E-kur of Enlil, the chief
god of the pantheon.

Enlil leads Ur-Nammu and a worker to begin work on a new
temple.

Ur-Namma and the god Enlil, with the Tree of Life between
them. Detail from the "Ur-Namma Stele".

A limestone fragment of the stele of Ur-Namma Stele, (Ur III
Period) circa 2097-2080 B.C.

The stele of Ur-Namma is the only surviving monumental
artwork from that period. Originally, the stele was more than
ten feet in height, and depicted various scenes and aspects of
Ur kingship. On the right, we see a god holding a staff and coil.

Limestone Fragment
from the Ur-Namma
Stele, circa 2097-2080 B.C.

Ur-Nammu, a king, a law-giver, and builder of the Ziggurat of Ur.

Ur Nammu atop the Ziggurat at Ur: "a Tower Unto the Heavens".

Ur-Nammu Ziggurat Dedication.
"For his lady Inanna, Ur-Nammu, the mighty man, the king of
Ur, the king of Sumer and Akkad, built her temple."

In Ur, the Stela of Ur-Nammu (Above) has the crescent symbol placed at the top of the register of gods because the moon god was the head of the gods. Even bread was baked in the form of a crescent as an act of devotion to the moon-god.

Ursaĝ: Noun.
a-A fighter,
b-A warrior,
c-A brave soldier,
d-A hero.

Urtur: Noun. A small dog.

Uru: Noun.
a-Lands,
b-Territory,
c-Kingdom,
d-A town.

Uru$_2$^{ki}: Noun.
a-A town,
b-A city,
c-A dwelling,
d-A neighborhood,
e-A village,
f-A district.

Uru$_4$: Verb.
a-To cultivate,
b-To plow,
c-To work the field,
d-To prepare the soil,
e-To till.

Uru$_7$: Noun.
a-Parents,
b-Relatives,
c-Cousins.

Uru$_9$: Noun.
a-A support,
b-An assistance,
c-A contribution,

d-Help.

Urubarra: Noun.
a-The suburb,
b-The countryside,
c-The outskirts of the city.

Uruda: Noun. Copper.

Urudu: Noun.
a-A large pot,
b-A large metal container,
c-Copper,
d-Metal.

Urugal: Noun.
a-The underworld,
b-Hell,
c-The netherworld.

Ú-rum: Noun.
a-A property,
b-Belongings,
c-Possession,
d-Ownership.

Ùru-m: Noun.
a-Light,
b-A sparkle.

Úrum: Noun.
a-Parents,
b-Relatives,
c-Cousins.

Ur-ur: Noun.
a-Close combat,
b-Man-to-man combat,

c-Hand-to-hand,
d-A single fight between two men.

Uru-šà-ga: Noun.
a-The center of the city,
b-The interior of the city.

Uruzag: Noun.
a-Lands,
b-Territory,
c-Kingdom.
In Hungarian the words "Orszag" and "Ursag" mean lands.

Úš: Adjective. Deceased.

Us: Noun. A length measure.

Úš: Noun.
a-Blood,
b-Death.

Uš: Noun.
a-Foundation of an edifice,
b-The base,
c-Perimeter of a construction,
d-A construction site.

Ús: Verb.
a-To follow,
b-To drive,
c-To ride,
d-To attain,
e-To reach,
f-To load goods,
g-To establish boundaries,
h-To bring together.
i-To bind.

Úš: Verb.
a-To die,
b-To expire,
c-To murder,
d-To kill,
e-To prevent,
f-To halt.

Uš$_{11}$: Noun.
a-Poison,
b-A venom,
c-A curse,
d-A spell.

Uš$_{11}$: Noun.
a-Poison,
b-A venom,
c-A curse,
d-A spell,
e-A charm.

Uš$_4$: Noun.
a-A good judgment,
b-A wise decision,
c-A consideration,
d-A common sense.

Us$_5$: Verb.
a-To support,
b-To retain,
c-To reinforce,
d-To lift,
e-To carry.

Usan$_2$: Noun.
a-End of the day,
b-The evening.

Usar da-gi₄: Noun.
a-A neighbor,
b-An associate,
c-A friend.

Usar: Noun.
a-A neighbor,
b-An associate,
c-A friend.

Ušar: Noun.
a-A neighbor,
b-An associate,
c-A friend.

Ušbar: Noun. A lamb wool weaver.

Ušbar₂: Noun.
a-A father-in-law,
b-A mother-in-law.

Ušbar₃: Noun.
a-A father-in-law,
b-A mother-in-law.

Ušgíd-da: Noun.
a-A barn,
b-A storehouse,
c-A storage area for grain and cereals,
d-A granary.

Ú-si₄-an-na: Noun. Dusk.

Ussu: Noun. Eight.

Ussu₂,: Noun. Eight.

Ussu₃: Noun. Eight.

Sumerian winged dragon.
As depicted on the ritual Libation Cup of King Gudea of Lagash,
circa 2100 B.C. The bas-relief depicts Tiamat as a dragon
(Serpent-Dragon in the Akkadian-Sumerian clay tablets epics).

Ušu: Noun.
a-A dragon,
b-A sea serpent,
c-A snake,
d-A demon.

Usu: Noun.
a-Skill,
b-Talent,
c- Strength,
d-Knowledge,
e-Wisdom,
f-Power,
g-Authority,
h-Experience,
i-Know-how.

Ù-su: Noun.
a-Vigor,
b-Physical strength,
c-Power,
d-Manpower,
e-Labor force,
f-Task-force,
g-Energy.

Usu: Noun.
a-Vigor,
b-Physical strength,
c-Power,
d-Manpower,
e-Labor force,
f-Energy.

Ùšu: Noun. Thirty

Ušum: Noun.
a-dragon,
b-A sea serpent,
c-A snake,
d-A demon.

Ùšur: Noun.
a-A friend,

b-A neighbor.
c-An associate.

Usu-tuku: Adjective.
a-A powerful person,
b-A physically strong person,
c-A skilled man.

Ùtu-d: Verb.
a-To create,
b-To give birth,
c-To engender,
d-To produce.

Útug: Noun. A weapon.

Utug: Noun.
a-A demon,
b-A bad spirit,
c-A malevolent spirit.
d-A demonic creature.

Útug: Noun. A Weapon.

Utul$_2$: Noun.
a-A cooking pan,
b-A pot,
c-A cauldron.

Utul$_7$: Noun.
a-A cooking pan,
b-A pot,
c-A cauldron.

Ù-ù: Preposition.
a-Either this or that,
b-Or.

Ù-ur₅-re: Adverb.
a-All of this,
b-All of it.

Úz: Noun.
a-The side,
b-The length,
c-The elevation,
d-The height,
e-The measurement,
f-The distance,
g-The separation,
h-The edge, i-The corner,
j-The angle.

Úz: Verb.
a- To pursue,
b-To continue,
c-To follow,
d-To gather,
e-To join,
f-To bring together,
g-To move around,
h-To ride.

Uzu: Noun. The flesh.

Uzu₅: Noun.
a-The evening,
b-The sunset.

Uzud: Noun. A female goat.

Uzud-saĝ: Noun.
a-A leader,
b-A guide,
c-A commander,
d-A supervisor.

Uru$_{17}$ (ULU$_3$): Adjective.
a-Powerful,
b-Strong,
c-Mighty,
d-Giant,
e-High.

U$_{18}$(ULU$_3$)-ru: Adjective.
a-Powerful,
b-Mighty,
c-High,
d-Influential,
e-Lofty,
f-Giant.

Uru$_{16}$-n: Adjective.
a-Bright,
b-Alert,
c-Intelligent,
d-Brave,
e-Strong,
f-Influential,
g-Powerful.

Uru$_2$: Adjective.
a-Elevated,
b-Tall,
c-High.

Uru$_5$: Adjective.
a-Elevated,
b-Tall,
c-High.

Uru$_{18}$: Adjective.
a-Elevated,
b-Tall,
c-High,

d-Deep.

Ur5: Preposition. Pronoun.
a-This,
b-This way,
c-Thus,
d-So,
e-Then.

Ur5-gin7: Adverb. Preposition.
a-Like this,
b-Thus.

Ur$_5$-re, ur$_5$-e: Adverb. Preposition.
a-In such manner,
b-In this way,
c-Like this,
d-Thus.

Ur$_5$-šè-àm: Adverb. Preposition.
a-Because of this,
b-Thus,
c-Therefore,
d-Henceforth.

Uru$_{2,5,18}$: Noun.
a-A huge flood,
b-An immense thunderstorm.

Ušumgal: Noun. Adjective.
a-The lord of all,
b-The master of everything,
c-The ultimate master,
d-The great ruler.

*** *** ***

d**Udug:** Noun.
a-Entities,
b-Spirits,
c-Djinns,
d-Demons.

d**Utu:** Noun. The sun god.

The sun god Utu risin from beneath the earth, from the seal of
Adda, circa 2,350-2,100 B.C.

d**Utu-è:** Noun. The sunrise.

ĝiš **Ur-ure:** Verb.
a-To fight,
b-To take part in a competition,
c-To take part in a combat.

_{giš}**Ur:** Noun. Wood used in building bridges. Gisur in Arabic means a bridge.

_{giš}**Ùšub:** Noun. A brick mould.

_{Giš}**ù-suh₅:** Noun. A pine tree.

^{iti}**u₅-bí-gu₇:** Noun.
a-The calendar month 3 at Drehem,
b-The calendar month 4 during the Ur III period.

^{iti}**Ur:** Noun. The calendar month 7 during the Ur III period.

^{kuš}**ÙB:** Noun. A drum.

^{kuš}**Ummud:** Noun.
a-A water container,
b-A water bag made from animal skin.

*** *** ***

Z

Zà: Noun.
a-A boundary,
b-A frontier,
c-A limit.

Za: Noun.
a-A gem,
b-A precious stone.

Za: Pronoun. You.

Za: Verb.
a-To repeat the same noise,
b-To produce disturbing sound,
c-To keep on repeating the same movement or the same sound in a monotous manner.

Za: Verb.
a-To circulate,
b-To liquify.

Za$_2$: Noun.
a-A precious stone,
b-A gemstone,
c-A precious metal.

Zabar: Noun.
a-A vessel made from bronze,
b-Silverware,

71

c-A mirror,
d-Bronze.

Zabar-dab5: Noun.
a-An influential state official,
b-A powerful person appointed by the royal court.

Zabar-šu: Noun. A mirror.

Zadim: Noun.
a-A jewelery designer,
b-Bracelets and rings maker,
c-A precious gem artisan,
d-A mason,
e-A stone cutter.

Sumerian/Mesopotamian jewelry.

Headdress, made from lapis lazuli, gold, and carnelian. Early
Dynastic II, circa 2,600 B.C.

Zag: Noun.
a-A frontier, usually determined by a Kudurru (Boundary stone),
b-A border,
c-A boundary,
d-A limit,
e-An outskirt,
 f-Outer-limit,
g-A perimeter.

A Sumerian Kudurru (Boundary stone).

Zàg: Verb. To select.

Zagìn: Adjective.
a-Bright,
b-Sunny,
c-Shinning,
d-Clear,
e-Sparkling,
f-Intact,
g-Clean,
h-Pure.

Zaggalla: Noun.
a-A seat,
b-A chair,
c-A place or a seating reserved to a dignitary.

Zaggula: Noun.
a-A seat,
b-A chair.

Zagše$_3$: Noun.
a-Authority,
b-Power,
c-Strength.

Zagša$_4$: Noun.
a-Authority,
b-Power,
c-Strength.

Zagšuš: Verb.
a-To engrave,
b-To cause a seal,
c-To mark or document a property using a stamp-seal.

Sumerian stamp-seals.

Zagtag: Verb.
a-To deny,
b-To refuse,
c-To reject,
d-To put aside.

Zaguru: Noun.
a-A suburb,
b-A district,
c-A neighborhood outside the city.

Zagús: Verb.
 a-To push away,
b-To put aside.

Zàh: Noun.
a-An escapee,
b-A fugitive,
c-A vagabond.

Záh: Verb.
a-To run away,
b-To evade,
c-To hide,
d-To escape,
e-To flee.

Zàkéš: Verb.
a-To glue,
b-To bind,
c-To fasten,
d-To attach,
e-To join.

Zal: Adjective.
a-Bright,
b-Clean,
c-Pure,

d-Sparkling.

Zalag₂: Adjective.
a-Bright,
b-Clean,
c-Pure,
d-Sparkling

Zalag₂: Noun. Light.

Zalag₂: Verb.
a-To glitter,
b-To shine,
c-To clean,
d-To polish.

Zalamĝar: Noun.
a-A hut,
b-A tent.

Zaltu: Noun. Sumerian/Akkadian/Babylonian.
Akkadian and Babylonian goddess of strife.
Zaltu was created by Ea, the King of the Gods, to personify the destructive side of the Goddess Ishtar.

Zàmí: Noun.
a-An homage,
b-A tribute,
c-A praise,
d-Reverence.

Zàmídu11: Verb.
a-To pay tribute,
b-To sing the praise of somebody,
c-To glorify,
d-To revere,
e-To recognize,

f-To pay respect.

Zàmu-k: Noun.
 a-The end of the year,
b-The end of the season.

Zàñ: Verb. To choose.

Zapa-áĝ: Noun.
a-A noise,
b-A sound,
c-A whisper.

Zar: Noun.
a-A small hill,
b-A pile,
c-A bundle,
d-A hay stack,
e-A mound.

Zàr: Noun.
a-A small hill,
b-A pile,
c-A bundle,
d-A hay stack,
e-A mound.

Zara$_5$: Verb.
a-To wrap,
b-To cover,
c-To roll,
d-To spin.

Zàšú: Verb.
a-To leave a mark,
b-To cause a seal,
c-To engrave the name of an owner, a brand, a label, or to mark an ownership's right.

79

Zàšu₄: Verb.
a-To leave a mark,
b-To cause a seal,
c-To engrave the name of an owner or mark an ownership's right.

Zàtag Verb.
a-To deny,
b-To put aside,
c-To impress.

Zé: Verb.
a-To cut,
b-To trim.

Zerpanitum: Noun. Sumerian/Akkadian.
Zerpanitum (Zer-banitum) was Marduk's consort. She was also called Aru'a in an inscription of Antiochus Soter (280-260 B.C.) She was identified with Aruru, the Anunnaki goddess who created mankind.
She was also called "the lady of the abyss". Zerpanitum was one of the most important goddesses in the Babylonian pantheon.

Zilugal: Noun.
a-A pledge,
b-An oath,
 c-A promise.

Zi: Adjective.
a-Tall,
b-Elevated.

Zí: Adjective. Bitter.

Zi: Noun. A breath.

Zi: Noun.
a-A divider,

b-A wall,
c-A separation.

Zi: Verb.
a-To destroy,
b-To ruin,
c-To erase,
 d-To decimate.

Zib$_2$: Noun.
a-A mark,
b-A sign,
c-A seal.

Zid: Adjective.
a-Righteous,
b-Just,
c-Real,
d-Bona fide,
e-Proper,
f-Justified,
g-Lawful,
h-Legal.

Zid: Noun.
a-Trust,
b-Confidence,
c-Belief.

Zi-da: Adjective.
a-Truthful,
b-Accurate,
c-Just,
d-Righteous.

Zidu: Adjective.
a-Truthful,
b-Accurate,

c-Just,
d-Righteous.

Zìg: Noun.
a-A divider,
b-A wall,
c-A separation.

Zi-g: Verb.
a-To change,
b-To remove,
c-To alter,
d-To stand up.

Zìg: Verb.
a-To incite,
b-To stand up.

Ziggurat: Noun. Sumerian/Akkadian.
Ziggurat derived from the Old Babylonian word "Zaquru", which means:
- **a-** To be high;
- **b-** Elevated;
- **c-** Raised up.

The Akkadian/Sumerian word Ziggurat means:
- **1-** The top of a mountain;
- **2-** A staged tower.

The ziggurat symbolized the link between heaven and Earth. For example:
- **a-**The ziggurat of Sippar was called the "Temple of the Stairway to Pure Heaven."
- **b-** The ziggurat of Nippur was called the "House binding Heaven and Earth."
- **c-** The ziggurat of Larsa was called the "Temple linking Heaven and Earth."
- **d-** The ziggurat of Babylon was called the "Temple of the Foundation Platform of Heaven and Earth." So on.

Ziggurat of Nanna in Ur.

One of the most famous and biggest ziggurats was in Babylon; it was dedicated to Marduk, and was called Etemenanki, which means "House platform of Heaven and Earth."

Enlil Ziggurat.

A mud brick ziggurat at Ur, erected by King Ur-nammu.

A mud brick ziggurat at Ur (Where Abraham came from) was erected by King Ur-nammu around 2100 B.C. He dedicated it to the moon-god Nanna. It was an immense compound consisting of three terraced stages. It rose 75 feet.
Similar ziggurats and temples were everywhere in Mesopotamia, and Abraham was familiar with the deities to whom they were built. Being a citizen of Ur, he had no choice but to worship the Anunnaki's deities, and revere Enki, Elil and their whole pantheon. By doing so, Abraham has already found his "God".

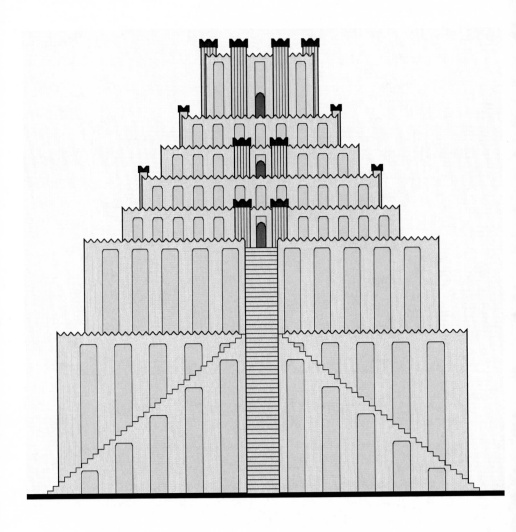

Reconstruction of the Etemenanki, approximately 273 feet in height.

Enlil's ziggurat

The ziggurat of Enlil in Nippur, Iraq.

Close up of the baked bricks and bitumen mortar of the ziggurat at Ur
"They used brick instead of stone, and tar for mortar" for the Tower of Bible (Gn 11:3).

Ziggurat of Ur.

Remains of the Ziggurat of Eanna.

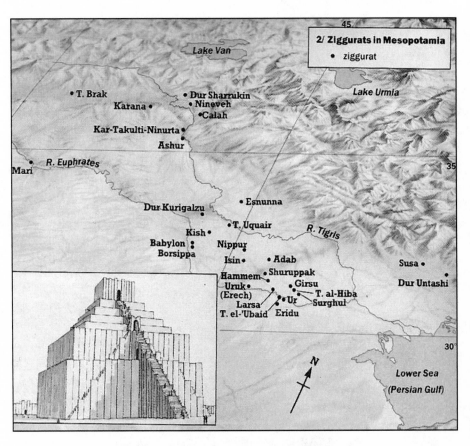

Ziggurat Locations in the Ancient Near East.

Blueprint of a typical Babylonian Ziggurat.

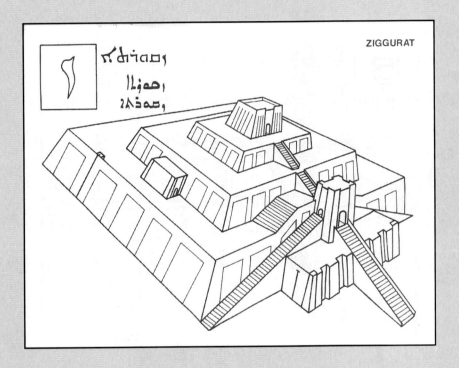

A ziggurat

Zigi₄: Verb.
a-To take it easy,
b-To relax,
c-To slow down.

Zi-ikrum: Adjective.
a-A sage,
b-A wise man,
c-An old man.

Zi-ir: Verb.
a-To remove,
b-To delete,
c-To hide,
d-To level,
e-To damage,
f-To destroy.

Zíl: Verb.
a-To embellish,
b-To ameliorate,
c-To improve.

Zilugal: Noun.
a-A pledge,
b-An oath,
c-A promise.

Zi-mah: Adjective.
a-Legal,
b-Bona fide,
c-Authentic,
d-Lofty,

Zipà: Verb.
a-To promise,
b-To swear,
c-To ascertain.

93

Zišàĝál: Verb.
a-To incite,
b-To energize,
c-To stimulate,
d-To re-inforce,
e-To increase,
f-To welcome,
g-To encourage,
h-To enhance.

Zišàĝál: Noun.
a-Stimulation,
b-Inspiration,
c-Creativity,
d-Encouragement,
e-Enhancement.

Zú: Noun. A tooth.

Zu: Noun.
a-Wisdom,
b-Awareness,
c-High level of intelligence,
d-Knowledge,
e-Remarkable expertise.

Zu: Noun. Akkadian/Sumerian/Old Babylonian.
Also known as "Anzu", and"Pazuzu".
In Sumero-Akkadian mythology, Zu is a divine demon-bird (half man and half bird), also referred to as Imdugud or Anzu.
He stole the "Tablets of Destiny" from the Anunnaki god Enlil and hid them on the top of a mountain.
According to one passage in the Akkadian/Sumerian tablets, Marduk killed the bird, but in another passage, the Anunnaki goddess Ninurta killed him. Yet, in an old version of the Babylonian story, Ea/Enki, father of Marduk destroyed Zu.

94

A fascinating depiction of a divine bird is provided in the Book of Ramadosh. Ulema Al Moutawalli translated an old Ana'kh text referring to that "Magical Bird", and stated that a group of Al Mounawariin did in fact used the bird as a tool to forecast future events, already recorded in a zone which he called "Mouka-Ballah", which means a "Parallel Distance".

Gilgamesh killing the bird Anzu.

From left to right: 1-Ishtar, 2-Gilgamesh killing the bird Anzu who stole the Tablet of Destiny, 3-Enkidu with his right foot pushing down Anzu to the ground.

A scene from the Epic of Gilgamesh.

Enkidu on the left with a spear, and on the right Gilgamesh
killing the bird-man Anzu, with a dagger.

Zu: Verb.
a-To comprehend,
b-To learn,
c-To know,
d-To declare,
e-To find,
f-To instruct,
g-To teach.

Zúgub: Verb.
a-To eat,
b-To bite.

Zuh: Verb. To steal.

Zuha: Adjective. Stolen

Zur: Noun.
a-A ritual offering,
b-An hymn,
c-A prayer,
d-A religious chant,
e-A ritual sacrifice during a cult ceremony.

Zur: Verb.
a-To cut,
b-To break.

*** *** ***

^{giš}**zà-mí:** Noun. A harp.

^{iti}**Zíz-a:** Noun. The calendar month 11 at Nippur during Ur III.

^{na4}**Za-gìn:** Noun.
a-Lapis lazuli,
b-A precious stone.

BIBLIOGRAPHIES AND REFERENCES

1-Ludwig Koehler and Walter Baumgartner. The Hebrew and Aramaic Lexicon of the Old Testament; Aramaic Lexicon & Supplementary Bibliography. Brill, University of Manchester, 2000

2-Michael Sokoloff. A Dictionary of Jewish Palestinian Aramaic of the Byzantine Period. The Bar-Ilan University Press and The Johns Hopkins University Press. Publications of The Comprehensive Aramaic Lexicon Project. 2003

3-A J Maclean. Dictionary of the Dialects of Vernacular Syriac. Gorgias Press LLC. 2003

4-M. Rubens Duval. Les Dialectes Néo-Araméens de Salamas. Textes sur l'état actuel de la Perse et contes populaires. Gorgias Press LLC. 2007

5-Handbuch der Orientalistik, Leiden, E.J. Brill. Berlin, Editions: 1953, 1954, 1995

6-Lexicon in Veteris Testamenti Libros, Ludwig Koehler, Walter Baumgartner, Berlin, New York, 1958

7-Cursus Scrip. Sac., Hummelauer, London, 1895

8-Naissance de L'Ecriture Cuneiformes et Hieroglyphes. Editions de la réunion des musées nationaux, Paris, 1982.

9-Bulletin of the School of Oriental and African Studies, University of London, Volumes 59, 60, No. 2 , London, 1997.

10-Shams Al Maaref Al Koubra, Damascus, 1300

11- Helden en goden van Sumer: Een keuze uit de heroische en mythologische dichtkunst van her Oude Mesopotamie. Marc Van De Mieroop. American Oriental Society, 2001

12-Hamito-Semitic Etymological Dictionary: Materials for a Reconstruction by Vladimir E. Orel; Olga V. Stolbova, Moscow, 1953

13-Die Keilschriftzeichen der Wirtschaftsurkunden von Ur III nebst ihren charakteristischsten Schreibvarianten, Keilschrift-Paläographie; Heft 2, Nikolaus Schneider, Rom: Päpstliches Bibelinstitut.1935

14-Dirasat Kitab Rama-Dosh, Dmascus, 1932

15-Legends of the Old Testament Characters Baring-Gould, 1871.

16-Sinai and Palestine; Stanley.

17-Hethitisches Keilschrift-Lesebuch. J. Friedrich. Heidelberg, 1960

18-Testi lessicali monolingui della biblitheca L. 2769. Materiali Epigrafici di Ebla 3. Napoli: Istituto universitario orientale di Napoli, Giovanni Pettinato. Napoli, 1981

19-Recherches Sur L'origine de L'écriture Cunéiforme. Thureau Dangin. Paris, 1898

20-Répertoire Commenté des Signes Présargoniques Sumériens de Lagash. Y. Rosengarten, Paris, 1967

21-The Sumerian Dictionary of the University of Pennsylvania Sjöberg, Åke, Editor. With the collaboration of Hermann Behrens, Antoine Cavigneaux , Barry L. Eichler, Margaret W. Green, Erle Leichty, Darlene M. Loding, Steve Tinney. Philadelphia: The Babylonian Section of the University Museum; 1995.

22-Sources in the History of Mathematics and the Physical Sciences Springer-Verlag, New York, Berlin, 1983.

23-Mathematical Cuneiform Texts. American Oriental Series. Neugebauer, Otto, and A. J. Sachs, American Oriental Society, New Haven, 1946.

24-First Impressions, Cylinder Seals in the Ancient Near East. Dominique Collon. British Museum Publications, London, 1987.

25-The Curse of Agade. Jerrold S. Cooper. John Hopkins University Press, 1983.

26-House Most High, The temples of Ancient Mesopotamia. A.R. George, 1993.

27-A History of the Babylonians and Assyrians, George Stephen Goodspeed, The Scribner Press, 1902

28-Assyrian Dictionary, Volumes 1, 2, 3. Edwin Norris, Willians and Norgate, London, Edinburgh, 1870. Elibron Classics, 2005

29-Die Keilschrift von Boghazköi. E. Forrer. Leipzig, 1922

Before The Muses: An Anthology Of Akkadian Literature. Benjamin Foster. CDL Press, 3rd edition, 2005
30-Manuel D'epigraphie Akkadienne. René Labat. Geuthner, Deuxieme Edition. Paris, 1959
31-Liste der Archaischen Keilschriftzeichen.A. Deimel, Berlin, 1922
32-Anunnaki Encyclopedia, Volumes 1, 2. M. de Lafayette, Times Square Press, New York, London, Paris, and Amazon.com Publishing Company, California, 2008
33-The American Journal of Semitic Languages and Literatures, Vol. 31, No. 3 . April 1915
34-The Sumerian Inscriptions of Sin-Gâšid, King of Erech. George S. Duncan. University of Chicago Press, Chicago. 1915
35-Pantheon Babylonicum. Nomina Deorum e Textibus Cuneiformibus Excerpta et Ordine Alphabetico Distributa. Theophile James Meek. University of Chicago Press. Chicago 2001
36-History of Babylonia and Assyria. Volume 1. Robert William Rogers. Eaton & Mains. 1901.
37-Mémoires de l'Académie des Inscriptions et Belles Lettres, Raoul Rochette. Paris, 1848
38-The Literature of Ancient Sumer. Jeremy Black, Graham Cunningham, E. Robson, G. Zolyami. Oxford University Press, 2006
39-Mesopotamisches Zeichenlexikon. R. Borger, Münster, 2003
40-The Harps that Once: Sumerian Poetry in Translation. Thorkild Jacobsen. Yale University Press, 1997
41-Archaische Texte aus Uruk. Adam Falkenstein. Berlin-Leipzig, 1936
42The Invention of Cuneiform, Jean-Jacques Glassner, Johns Hopkins University Press, 2003
43-Kiraat Fil' Fikr Al Rouhi. Ulema, Cairo, 1012
44-Ugaritic Narrative Poetry. Simon B. Parker. CDL Press. 2005 Sumerian Grammar. Handbook of Oriental Studies. Dietz Otto Edzard. Society of Biblical Literature, 2003
45-A Manual of Sumerian Grammar and Texts. John L. Hayes. Undena Publications, 2000

46-Reading the Past Cuneiform. C.B. F. Walker. University of California Press, 1987

47-The Descendants of Adam; Creation to Patriarchs, Geikie, 1890.

48-The Legends of Genesis, Gunkel, 1901.

49-The Problems of the Old Testament, Driver 1906.

50-The Bible, the Koran, and the Talmud, Weil, 1846.

51-Encyclopedia Britannica, 1952, 2007

52-Encyclopedie Larousse, Paris, 2004

53-Catholic Encyclopedia, 2008

54-Assyrian Grammar. A.H. Sayce. Wipf & Stock Publishers, London, New York, 1900

55-Grammar of the Phoenician Language. Zellig Harris. Eisenbrauns, Berlin, New York. 1936

56-A Phoenician-Punic Grammar (Handbook of Oriental Studies). Charles Krahmalkov. Brill, London, Brill, 2000

57-A Dictionary of Jewish Babylonian Aramaic of the Talmudic and Geonic Periods. Michael Sokolof. The Bar-Ilan University Press and The Johns Hopkins University Press, 2003

58-A Comparative Semitic Lexicon of the Phoenician and Punic languages. Richard S. Tomback. Scholars Press for the Society of Biblical Literature, 1978

59-Geschichte der Vorgeschichtsforschung. Herbert Kuhn. De Gruyter, 1976

61-La Mésopotamie : de Sumer à Babylone. Erica Hunter. Casterman, 1995.

62-Life in Ancient Mesopotamia. Shilpa Mehta-Jones. Crabtree Publishing Company, 2004

63-Mésopotamie. L'Apparition de L'Etat. Jean-Daniel Forest.Paris-Méditéranée, 1996.

64-Dictionnaire de la Bible, Palis, Paris, 1846

65-Aramaic Studies During the Past Thirty Years. F. Rosenthal The Journal of Near Eastern Studies. Chicago, 1978

66-First Impressions, Cylinder Seals in the Ancient Near East. Dominique Collon. British Museum Publications. London, 1987

67-Per aspera ad astra. L'apprentissage du Cunéiforme à Sippar-Amnanum pendant la période Paléobabylonienne Tardive. Ghent, University of Ghent, 2002

68-Edubba'a und Edubba'a-Literatur: Rätsel und Lösungen. Zeitschrift für Assyriologie. Konrad Volk, 2002

69-Leistung und Grenze sumerischer und babylonischer Wissenschaft." Die Welt als Geschichte Die Eigenbegrifflichkeit der babylonischen Welt in: Sonderausgabe Wissenschaftliche Buchgesellschaft, WolframVon Soden, Darmstadt, 1965

70- L. Kriss-Rettenbeck and M. Liedtke (eds.): Keilschrift und Schulen in Mesopotamien und Ebla. 1986

71-Die Entwicklung der Naturwissenschaften und des naturwissenschaftlichen Unterrichts in Mesopotamien. J.G. Prinz Hohenzollern, M. Liedtke (eds., 1988

72-Lenticular Exercise School Texts. Texts in the Iraq Museum 10/1. Baghdad: The State Organization of Antiquities. Abdul-Hadi Al-Fouadi. Baghdad, 1979.

73-Recherches au pays d'Aštata. Emar VI. Textes Sumériens et Accadiens. Éditions Recherche sur les Civilizations. Arnaud, Daniel. Paris, 1986

74-Sumerian Lexical Texts from the Temple School of Nippur. Oriental Institute Publications 11. Chicago: Oriental Institute. Edward Chiera. Chicago, 1929

75-Die lexikalischen Listen der archaischen Texte aus Uruk. Archaische Texte aus Uruk 3. Englund, R.K., and H.J. Nissen Berlin: Gebr. Mann, 1939

76-Akkadische Logogramme, Goettinger Arbeitshefte zur Altorientalischen Literatur (Gaal) Heft 4, Wolfgang Schramm. Goettingen, 2003

77-Die Lexikalischen Tafelserien der Babylonier und Assyrer in den Berliner Museen. Berlin: Staatliche Museen. Matouš, Lubor and Wolfram von Soden. Berlin, 1933

78-Schulunterricht in Babylonien im ersten Jahrtausend v. Chr. Alter Orient und Altes Testament 275. Ugarit-Verlag: Münster. Petra D. Gesche. Berlin, 2001

79-Lexicography: Sumerological Studies/Assyriological Studies. Miguel Civil. The University of Chicago Press, Chicago, 1976.

80- Mesopotamia. Gwendolyne Leick. Penguin, 2003

81-Manuel d'Épigraphie Akkadienne. R. Labat and F. Malbran-Labat. Paris, 1995

82-Bulletin of The International Congress of Assyriology and Near Eastern Archaeology. Moscow, Saint Petersburg, 2007
83-A Dictionary of Jewish Babylonian Aramaic of the Talmudic and Geonic Periods. Michael Sokolof. The Bar-Ilan University Press and The Johns Hopkins University Press, 2003
84-The Sumerians: Their History, Culture, and Character. Samuel Noah Kramer. University Of Chicago Press. Chicago, 1971.
85-Altorientalische Forschungen, Winckler. Keilinschrift. Bibl., Berlin. 2000
86-Gli Eponimi Medio-Assiri, Claudio Saporetti. Roma, 1979.
87-Les sattuku dans l'Esumesa durant la période d'Isin et Larsa. Rene Marcel Sigrist, 1984
88-Catalogue of Artifacts in the Babylonian Collection of the Lowie Museum of Anthropology, Yoko Tomabechi. 1984
89-Old Babylonian Texts from Kish Conserved in the Istanbul Archaeological Museums, V. Donbaz and N. Yoffee. 1986.
90-The Oriental Institute Excavations at Selenkahiye, Syria: Terra-Cotta Figurines and Model Vehicles, Harold Liebowitz; M. van Loon, Ed. 1988.
91-The Sumerian Language: An Introduction to Its History and Grammatical Structure. M.L. Thomsen. Copenhagen, 1984
92-Late Babylonian Texts of the Oriental Institute D. Weisberg, 1991
93-Gli Opifici di Urkesh: Conservazione e restauro a Tell Mozan, Atti della Tavola Rotondo tenuta presso L'Opificio delle Pietre Dure, Firenze, 1999
94-Cuneiform Mathematical Texts as a Reflection of Everyday Life in Mesopotamia. K.R. Nemet-Nejat. American Oriental Series. New Haven, 1993
95-The Domestication of Equidae in Third Millennium B.C. Mesopotamia, Juris Zarens. 2008.
96-Notes de Graphie et de Phonétique Sumériennes. R. Jestin, Paris, 1965
97-Šumerisches Lexikon. A. Deimel. Rome, 1947
98-Chicago Assyrian Dictionary. University of Chicago, Chicago, 2000

99-Studies in the Chronology and Regional Style of Old Babylonian Cylinder Seals, Lamia al-Gailani Werr. 1988
100- The Early History of Indo-European Languages. Thomas V. Gamkrelidze and V. Ivanov, Scientific American. 1990
101-The Semites in Ancient History. Alexander Badawy, J. Near Eastern Studies, 1963
102-The Protohistoric Ethnography of Western Asia. Daniel G. Brinton, American Philosophical Society. 1895
103-The Races of Europe. Carleton Stevens Coon. Macmillan Co., New York, 1939, 1954
104-Das erste Auftreten der Indogermanen in Vorderasien. Mitteilungen der anthropologischen Gesellschaft Wien (MAGW).1928
105- John Coles. Caxton's History of the World. New Caxton Library Series. London, 1969
106- B. S. Dahiya. Jats: The Ancient Rulers. B. S. Dahiya. Sterling Publishers Pvt. Ltd. New Delhi, India, 1980.
107-B.S.Dehiya and Vishveshvaranand.The Mauryas: Their Identity. Indological Journal. New Delhi. 1979
108-Die Arier in den nahoestlichen Quellen des 3 und 2. Jahrtausends..Jahanshah.Derakhshani..Internat'l.Publication.of Iranian Studies. 1999
109-Earliest Traces of the Aryan: Evidence from the 4th and 3rd Millennium B.C. Jahanshah Derakhshani, Iran & the Caucasus, vol. V. 2001
110-The Kurdish Question.W.G.Elphinston, International Affairs Royal Institute of International Affairs. 1946
111-Hurrians and Subarians. Ignace. J. Gelb. The Oriental Institute of the Univ. of Chicago: Studies in Ancient Oriental Civilizations. University of Chicago Press, 1944
112-The Aryan Origin of the Alphabet. L.A. Waddell. Royal Anthropological Institute. London University, London; Luzac & Co., London, 1927. Christian Book Club of America. California, 1998.
113-The Makers of Civilization in Race and History. L .A. Waddell, Luzac & Co., 1929. S. Chand & Company. New Delhi, 1986

114-The Sumerians. Charles Leonard Woolley. W. W. Norton, New York, 1929, 1965. Barnes & Noble, 1995

115-Before the Bible: The Common Background of Greek and Hebrew Civilisations. Cyrus H. Gordon, Collins. London, 1962

116-Die Kurden. Ferdinand Hennerbichler. Mosonmagyarovar, Slovakia, 2004

117-The First Indo-Europeans in History. Walter B. Henning, and G.L. Ulmen. The Hague/Paris/New York, 1978

118-The Early History of Babylonia. Henry H. Howorth. The English Historical Review, Vol. 16.1901

119-History Of Turkish Occupation Of Northern Kurdistan. Eric Jensen. Third World Politics. 1996

120-The Sumerians. Samuel Noah Kramer, Univ. of Chicago Press. Chicago, 1963.

121-Akkadian Origins. D. D. Luckenbill. The American Journal of Semitic Languages and Literatures. 1923

122-Das Volk Ohne Anwalt: Geschichte, Kultur, Literatur und Religion in Kurdistan-eine Einfuehrung," Nazif Telek. Der Auslaenderbeauftragte.der.Thueringer.Landesregierung, Weimardruck Weimar. 2003

123-Mesopotamian Origins, The Basic Population of the Near East. E.A.Speiser, Philadelphia, London. 1930

124-Patriarchal Palestine. Archibald Henry Sayce. Society for Promoting Christian Knowledge, London. 1895

125-Journal Asiatique, Paris, 1863

126-The Aramaic language: Its distribution and subdivisions Klaus Beyer. Vandenhoeck und Ruprecht, Göttingen: 1986

127-An Introduction to Syriac Studies. Sebastian Brock. Gorgias Press Piscataway, NJ, 2006

128-First Studies in Syriac. John Healy. Univ. of Birmingham, Sheffield Academic Press, 1980

129-Indo-European and the Indo-Europeans: A reconstruction and historical analysis of a Proto-language and a Proto-culture. Gamkrelidze, Thomas V. & Vjacheslav V. Ivanov. Mouton de Gruyter. Berlin & New York. 1995

130-Winfred Lehmann. A Reader in Nineteenth Century Historical Indo-European Linguistics.. Indiana University Press, 1967

131-Encyclopedia of Indo-European Culture. J.P. Mallory, &
Douglas Q. Adams. London & Chicago, 1997
132-The Hittite Language. V. Ivanov Moscow, 1963
133-Common Indo-European, Proto-Slavic and Anatolian 134-
Language Systems. V. Ivanov. Moscow, 1964
134-T. Gamkrelidze , and V. Ivanov. Indo European Language
and Indo Europeans. Moscow, 1984
135-The Experience of the Comparative Studies of Hitto-Luwian
Languages. L. Bajun. Moscow, 1990
136- L. Bajun. The Language of Hittite Hieroglyphs. Moscow.
1986.
137-Anthropological Observations in South Arabia. Bertram
Thomas. Royal Anthropological Institute of Great Britain and
Ireland. 1932.
138-Karin and Karineh. W. Blackman. Royal Anthropological
Institute of Great Britain and Ireland. 1926
139-The Baladi Curative System of Cairo, Egypt. Springer.
Netherlands, 1988
140-The Fellahin of Upper Egypt, Winifred S Blackman, AUC.
Cairo, 1927
141-The Decipherment of Arabic Talismans. Tewfik Canaan.
Beirut, 1937
142-Mesopotamisches Zeichenlexicon. Rykle Borger, 2003.
143-Manuel d'épigraphie akkadienne. René Labat. Paris, 1988
144-A Concise Dictionary of Akkadian Black, Jeremy A., George,
Andrew and Postgate, Nicholas, 2000.
145-Assyrisches Handwörterbuch. Friedrich Delizsch, 1896
146-A Grammar of Akkadian. John Huehnergard, 2000
147-Hethitisches Zeichenlexikon.Inventar und Interpretation
der Keilschriftzeichen aus den Bogazkoy-Texten. Christel Ruster
and Erich Neu Harrassowitz. Verlag, 1989
148-The Sumerian Language. An Introduction to Its History and
Grammatical Structure, 2nd edition, Mesopotamia: Copenhagen
Studies in Assyriology. Marie-Louise Thomsen. Akademisk.
Forlag, 2001
149-Sketch of Neo-Assyrian Grammar. Jaakko Hameen Anttila,
2000
150-A Manual of Akkadian. David Marcus. 1978.

151-The Chicago Assyrian Dictionary. Leo Oppenheim. Chicago, 2000

152-The Helsinki Neo-Assyrian Dictionary. Simo Parpola, 2005

153-Syriac Dictionary Abed Dawod. 2005

154-Sumerian Grammar. Handbook of Oriental Studies, Part One: The Ancient Near East and Middle East. D. O. Edzard Brill Academic Publishers, 2003

155-A Manual of Sumerian Grammar and Texts Aids and Research Tools in Ancient Near Eastern Studies. John L. Hayes Undena Publications, 2000

156-Grundriss der akkadischen Grammatik, Analecta Orientalia. Wolfram von Soden Biblical Institute Press, Editrice Pontificio Istituto Biblico, 1995

157-A Grammar of Akkadian John Huehnergard. Harvard Semitic Studies, Harvard Semitic Museum, Eisenbrauns, 2000

158-Etymological Dictionary of the Hittite Inherited Lexicon. Alwin Kloekhorst. Brill, Netherlands, 2007

159-ADictionary of Ancient Near Eastern Mythology. Gwendolyn Leick. Routledge. New York,1998

160-Journal of the American Oriental Society. Erle Leichty. 1975

161-The Mystics of Islam. Reynold A. Nicholson. 2002.

162-The Sufi Orders in Islam. J. Spencer Trimingham. Oxford University Press. 1971.

163-Het Babylonische Nieuwjaarsfeest Bulletin van het Vooraziatisch Egyptisch genootschap Ex Oriente Lux 36/1. K. van der Toorn, 1990

164-A.R. George, "E-sangil and E-temen-anki, the Archetypal Cult-centre?" in: J. Renger, Babylon: Focus mesopotamischer Geschichte, Wiege früher Gelehrsamkeit, Mythos in der Moderne. A.R. George. Saarbrücken, 1999

165-Der Tempelturm Etemenanki in Babylon. Hansjörg Schmid. Mainz, 1995

166-Der Turmbau zu Babel. Band I: Der babylonische Turm in der historischen Überlieferung, der Archäologie und der Kunst. Seipel Wilfried. Graz , 2003

167-Annals of Tiglath Pileser; Nimrud Obelisk, Shalmaneser; Botta's Monument de Ninive. Journal Asiatique, Paris, 1863

168-Genesis of the Grail Kings. Laurence Gardner. Bantam Press, NY, 1999
169-Kautzsch-Gesentius Hebräische Grammatik. Leipzig, 1896
170-The Asiatic Journal. Sir Henry Rawlinson, 1864
171-Cuneiform Parallels to the Old Testament. R.W. Rogers. London, 1912
172-Cuneiform Inscriptions of Western Asia, Vol. I, plates 17 to 27. Professor Oppert. London 1865-66
173-Histoire des Empires de Chaldée et d'Assyrie: Extrait des Annales de Philosophie Chrétienne, tome. IX, London, Paris, 1865
174-The Texts of the Ugaritic Data Bank. Jesús-Luis Cunchillos, Juan-Pablo Vita and José-Ángel Zamora, Gorgias Press, 2005
175-The Ugaritic Textbook, Revised Edition. Cyrus Gordon. Gorgias Press, 1998
176-Sumerian Lexicon. John Halloran. Logogram Publishing. 2006
177- Mitchell Dahood. Ugaritic-Hebrew Philology.. 1965
178- Ernest R. Martinez, S.J. Hebrew-Ugaritic Index to the Writings of Mitchell J. Dahood, volumes I and II. 1981
179-The Ras Shamra Parallels, volumes I, II and III. Stan Rummel and Loren Fisher, eds. 1981
180-The Old Testament in the Jewish Church Robertson Smith. 1892
181-Literature of the Old Testament. Driver. 1898
182-Literature of the Old Testament. Oesterley and Robinson.1934
183-Erith's Lucid synopsis in Gore's Commentary. 1928
184- J. W. Jack. The Ras Shamra Tablets. 1935
185- Assyrian Dictionary. E. Norris. Brompton, 1967
186-Dalman Der Gottesname und seine Geschichte. Berlin, l889
187-Stade. Biblische Theologie des Alten Testaments. Tübingen, 1905
188- Bâbil, the City of Witchcraft and Wine. The Name and Fame of Babylon in Medieval Arabic Geographical Texts. Caroline Janssen. Ghent, 1995
189-Is dit niet het grote Babylon, dat ik gebouwd heb? Bert van der Spek. 1990

190-Abd Allāh ibn Umar al-Dumayjī. Ism Allāh al-aʾẓam. 2000.
191-Muhammad 'Abd al-Rahīm. Manzūmah fī sirr ism Allāh al-aʿzam. Dār al-Mukhtārāt al-ʿArabīyah. Beirut. 1993.
192-Ahmad Al Buni. Shams al-Maʾaref al-Kubra. Cairo. 1928.
193-Pere Georges Anawati. Le Nom Supreme de Dieu, Atti del Terzo Congresso Di Studi Arabi e Islamici. Roma. 1966.
194-Bruce Metzger, Historical and Literary Studies: Pagan, Jewish and Christian, Brill. 1968
195-Samuel Noah Kramer, The Sumerians: Their History, Culture, and Character, Phoenix Books. 1971
196-H. A. Winkler. Siegel und Charaktere in der Muhammedanischen Zauberei. Berlin and Leipzig. 1930.
197-Ahmad Al Buni. Sharh Ism Allah al-aʾzam fi al-Ruhani. Al-Matbaʾat al-Mahmudiyyat al-Tujjariyyat bi'l-Azhar Cairo.1939.
198-William Foxwell Albright. Archaeology and the Religion of Israel, Westminster John Knox Press. 2006
199-Denis MacEoin. Rituals in Babism and Bahaism. I. B. Tauris. London. 1995.
200-Muhammad al-Gharawī. Al-Ism al-aʾẓam aw maʾārif al-basmala wa'l-ḥamdala. Beirut. 1998. Emile Savage-Smith. Magic and Divination in Early Islam. Ashgate. 2004.
201-Jessie Weston. From Ritual to Romance. Cosimo Classics. 2005
202-Sir James Frazer, The Golden Bough, 1906
203-John H. Randall, Hellenistic Ways of Deliverance and the Making of the Christian Synthesis, 1970
204-Eerdmans Dictionary of the Bible. David Noel Freedman, Allen C. Myers, Astrid B. Beck. Wm. B. Eerdmans Publishing Company, 2000
205-Roy Willis. World Mythology. Holt Paperbacks.1996
206-Edo Nyland. Linguistic Archaeology, Trafford Publishing. 2006
207-G. Johannes Botterweck. Theological Dictionary of the Old Testament, Wm. B. Eerdmans Publishing Company. 1981
208-Emmet Sweeney. Empire of Thebes Or Ages In Chaos Revisited, Algora Publishing. 2006

110

209-E. A. Speiser. Genesis: Introduction, Translation, and Notes, Anchor Bible. 1964)

210-David Fasold. The Ark of Noah, Wynwood Press, New York. 1988

211-Ilil Arbel. Maimonides: A Spiritual Biography, Crossroad 8th Avenue. 2001

212-Piotr Bienkowsky and Alan Millard. Dictionary of the Ancient Near East. University of Pennsylvania, Philadelphia, Press. 2000

213-Gwendolyn Leick. Who's Who in the Ancient Near East. Routledge, London. 1999

214-Franz Bardon. Initiation into Hermetics. Wuppertal. Ruggeberg.1971

215-Amélie Kuhrt. The Ancient Near East, c. 3,000-330 B.C., Routledge, London. 1995

216-International Journal of Astrobiology. Cardiff University. 2006

217- Mary Boyce. Textual sources for the study of Zoroastrianism, Manchester. 1984

218-Dione Fortune.The Mystical Qabala. Weiser Books. 2000

219-Roger L. W. Hints to Young Students of Occultism. The Theosophical Book Company. Albany, N.Y. 1909

220-Richard W. Bulliet. Conversion to Islam in the Medieval Period: An Essay in Quantitative History, Cambridge. Harvard. 1979

221-Black, Matthew & Rowley, H. H. Peake's Commentary on the Bible. New York. 1982

222-Roger L. W. Hints to Young Students of Occultism. The Theosophical Book Company. Albany, N.Y. 1909

223-Warren H. Carroll. Founding Of Christendom: History Of Christendom. Urbana, Illinois.1985

224-Maneckji Nusservanji Dhalla. History of Zoroastrianism, New York. 1938

225-Eliade, Mircea & Couliano, Ioan P. The Eliade Guide to World Religions, New York: Harper Collins. 1991

226-Regardie, I., Cicero. The Tree of Life: An Illustrated Study in Magic. St. Paul, Minn. Llewellyn Publications. 2001

227- Professor Wickramasinghe, Professor Bill Napier and Dr. Janaki Wickramasinghe. The Origin of Life in Comets.
228-Charles William King. Gnostics and their Remains Ancient and Mediaeval. Bell & Daldy, London. 1887
229-John Haldon. Byzantium in the Seventh Century: The Transformation of a Culture. Cambridge. 1997
230-Ali Akbar, Sarfaraz, and Bahman Firuzmandi. Mad Hakhamanishi Ashkani Sasani. Marlik. 1996.
231-Abdolhossein Zarinkoob. Ruzgaran: tarikh-i Iran az aghz ta saqut saltnat Pahlvi. Sukhan. 1999.
232-H. Börm. Prokop und die Perser. Untersuchungen zu den römisch-sasanidischen Kontakten in der ausgehenden Spätantike. Stuttgart. 2007
233-Timothy Freke, Peter Gandy.The Hermetica: The Lost Wisdom of the Pharaohs. Tarcher. 1999
234-Bart. D. Ehrman. Lost Christianities. Oxford University Press. 2003.
235-H. Bossert. Wie lange wurden hethitische Hieroglyphen geschrieben. Die Welt des Orients.1952
236-W. Wroth. Catalogue of the Greek coins of Galatia, Cappadocia and Syria.Tabel XIV-XV.1899
237-A. Christensen: Le règne du roi Kawadh et le communisme Mazdakite. Kopenhagen. 1925
238-C. Küthman. Bemerkungen zu einigen Münzen des hellenistischen Ostens. Schweizer MünzblätterI. 1950
239-A. H. Sayce. The Hittites: The Story of a Forgotten Empire. 1888
240-W. Wright. The Empire of the Hittites. London. 1886.
241-Roger Henry. Synchronized Chronology. N.Y. 2003
242-David George Hogarth. Kings of the Hittites. London. 1924
243-D. Luckenbill: Ancient Records of Assyria and Babylonia. London. 1926
244-Justo L González. A History of Christian Thought. Abingdon. 1970
245-W. Sundermann. Neue Erkenntnisse über die mazdakitische Soziallehre. In: Das Altertum. 1988
246-Hans Jonas. The Gnostic Religion. Beacon Press. 1963

247-Barbara Aland. Festschrift für Hans Jonas. Vandenhoeck & Ruprecht. 1978

248-H. Güterbock. Die historische Tradition und ihre literarische Gestaltung bei Babyloniern und Hethitern bis 1200", Zeitschrift für Assyrologie. Berlin. 1938

249- Rocco Errico, Michael Bazzi. Classical Aramaic. Noohra Foundation. 1992

250-Robert Hetzron. The Semitic Languages. Routledge. 2005

251-William M. Schniedewind, Joel H. Hunt.A Primer on Ugaritic: Language, Culture and Literature. Cambridge University Press. 2007

252-Otto Puchstein. Pseudohethitische Kunst. Berlin. 1890

253-G. Contenau: Ce Que Nous Savons des Hittites. Revue Historique, Vol. CLXXXVI. Paris. 1939

254-Dennis Pardee. Ritual and Cult at Ugarit : Writings from the Ancient World. Society of Biblical Literature. 2002

255-Harry Hoffner. Gary Beckman. Hittite Myths. Scholars Press. 1991

256-Morris Jastrow. The Civilization of Babylonia and Assyria. J. B. Lippincott Co., London. 1915

257-Elmer D Johnson. History of Libraries in the Western World. Metuchen, The Scarecrow Press, Inc., New Jersey. 1970.

258-A. T Olmstead. The History of Assyria. Charles Scribner's Sons, New York. 1923

259-Wayne A. Wiegand, G. Davis, Donald Jr. Encyclopedia of Library History. Garland Publishing, Inc., New York. 1994

260-Josh McDowell. The Best Of Josh McDowell. Thomas Nelson Publishers, Nashville. 1993

261-V. Ivanov. Common Indo-European, Proto-Slavic and Anatolian Language Systems. Moscow. 1963.

262-V. Ivanov The Hittite Language. Moscow, 1963.

263-T. Gamkrelidze, V. Ivanov. The Indo-European Language and Indo-Europeans. Moscow, 1984.

264-I. Bajun. The Experience of the Comparative Studies of Hitto-Luwian Languages. Moscow, 1990.

265-A. Korolev. Hitto-Luwian Languages. Languages of Asia and Africa, vol. 1. Moscow, 1976.

113

266-M. Fasmer. Etymological Dictionary of the Russian Language. Moscow, 1986.
267-Zellig Harris. Grammar of the Phoenician Language. Eisenbrauns, Berlin, New York. 1936
268-Charles Krahmalkov. A Phoenician-Punic Grammar (Handbook of Oriental Studies). Brill, London, Brill, 2000
269-William Ellis. The New Face of Baghdad. National Geographic 167, no. 1, 1985
270-Philip K. Hitti. Capital Cities of Arab Islam. University of Minnesota Press, Minneapolis. 1973
271- A.D Chadwick. "Precambrian Pollen in the Grand Canyona Reexamination" Origins. 1981.
272-Sandra Mackey. The Reckoning: Iraq and the Legacy of Saddam Hussein. W. W. Norton, New York. 2002
273-Phebe Marr. The Modern History of Iraq, 2d edition. Westview Press. Boulder, Colorado. 1985
274-John Munday Jr. Eden's Geography Erodes Flood Geology. Westminster Theological Journal 58:1. 1996
275-Alger F. Johns. The Short Grammar of Biblical Aramaic. Andrews University Press. Berrien Springs. 1972
276-Michael Maher. Targum Pseudo-Jonathan: Genesis. English translation of the Aramaic. Collegeville. Liturgical Press. 1992
277-C. Frohlich, J.A. Eddy Observed Relations Between Solar Luminosity and Radius (A paper presented at conference of the Committee of Space Research in Graz, Austria.1984
278-Martin McNamara. Targum Pseudo-Neofiti I: Exodus. Liturgical Press. 1994
279-Laurie Godfrey. Scientists Confront Creationism. W.W.Norton & Company. New York. 1983
280-Alan Hayward. Creation and Evolution. Bethany House Publishers. Minneapolis. 1985
281-Tim Berra. Evolution and the Myth of Creationism. Standford: University Press. 1990
282-G. Brent Dalrymple. Radiometric Dating, Geological Time, and the Age of the Earth: A Reply to 'Scientific Creationism Open-File Report U.S. Geological Survey. 1982

283-John Bowker. The Targums & Rabbinic Literature: An Introduction to Jewish Interpretation of Scripture. (Genesis). Cambridge University Press, Cambridge. 1969.
284-Glen Kuban. Sea-monster or Shark? An Analysis of a Supposed Plesiosaur Carcass Netted in 1977. National Center for Science Education Reports May/June. 1997
285-Alexander Sperber. The Bible in Aramaic, Brill,.1959.
286-John D Morris. The Young Earth. Master Books. Glen Forest. 1994
287-Marcus Jastrow. Hebrew Aramaic English Dictionary. Shalom Publications, New York. 1967.
288-Dick Fischer. The Origins Solution. Lima. Fairway Press. 1996.
289-Hugh Ross. Creation and Time. Navpress. Colorado Springs. 1994
290-Don Stoner. A New Look at an Old Earth. Harvest House. Eugene. 1997
291-Authur Strahler. Science and Earth History. Prometheus Books. Amherst. 1999
292-Paul Taylor. The Illustrated Origins Answer Book. Eden Communications. Gilbert. 1995
293-Van Till, Young & Menninga. Science Held Hostage. InterVarsity Press. Downers Grove. 1988
294-Christopher Weber. The Flaws of Flood Geology. Creation/Evolution. 1980
295-Daniel E. Wonderly. Neglect of geological Data: Sedimentary Strata Compared with Young-Earth Creationist Writings. Hatfield: Interdisciplinary Biblical Research Institute. 1987
296-L.R. Bailey. Wood From Mount Ararat: Noah's Ark? 1977
297-Robert Best. Noah's Ark and the Ziusudra Epic. Enlil Press. Fort Myers. 1999
298-F.F Bruce. Commentary on the Book of the Acts. Eerdmans. Grand Rapids. 1977
299-William Hallo. The Context of Scripture. Brill. 1997
300-Stephanie Dalley. Myths from Mesopotamia. Oxford University Press. New York. 1989

115

301-Dick Fischer. The Origins Solution. Fairway Press. Lima. 1996

302-Victor Hamilton. The Book of Genesis. Eerdmans. Grand Rapids. 1990

303-Alexander Heidel. The Gilgamesh Epic and the O.T. University Press. Chicago. 1966

304-Richard S. Hess. Splitting the Adam: The Usage of Adam in Genesis. Studies in the Pentateuch: Vetus Supplementum XLI. Leiden. Brill. 1990

305-Studies in the Personal Names of Genesis 1-11: Alter Orient und Altes Testament 234. Neukircher-Vluyn. Neukirchener.1993

306-Getting Personal: What Names in the Bible Teach Us. Bible Review. December, 1997

307-R.S Hess & D.T Tsumura. Inscriptions Before the Flood. Eisenbrauns. Winona Lake. 1994

308-Wayne Horowitz. The Isles of the Nations: Genesis X and Babylonian Geography" in Studies in the Pentateuch ed. by J. A. Emerton. Leiden. Brill. 1990

309-Thorkild Jacobsen. Mesopotamian Cosmic Geography. Eisenbrauns. Winona Lake. 1939

310-Isaac Kikawada & Arthur Quinn .The Sumerian King List. Chicago: University Press. Abingdon Press. Nashville. 1985

311-Lambert, W.G. and A. Millard. Atra-Hasis: The Babylonian Story of the Flood. Clarendon Press. Oxford. 1969

312-William Shea. Adam in Ancient Mesopotamian Traditions. AUSS. 1977

313-John Walton. The Antediluvian section of the Sumerian King List and Genesis. Asor. 1981

314-Zondervan. Ancient Israelite Literature in Its Cultural Context. Grand Rapids. 1989

315-Gordon Wenham. The Coherence of the Flood Narrative. 1978

316-Word Biblical Commentary: Genesis. Word Books. Waco. 1987

317-Claus Westermann. Genesis, Trans. by John Scullion. Fortress Press.Minneapolis. 1994

318-Daniel Wonderly. Neglect of Geological Data. Hatfield. IBRI. 1987

319-Ron Wyatt. Discovered: Noah's Ark! World Bible Society. Nashville. 1989

320-Oxford Classical Dictionary. Oxford. 1949

321-John Bowker. The Tarums & Rabbinic Literature. Cambridge University Press. 1969

322-Jacob Neusner. Genesis Rabbah Scholars Press. 1985

323-Sir Leonard Woolley. Ur of the Chaldees: A Record of Seven Years of Excavation. Rev. ed. Penguin. Harmondsworth. 1950.

324-The Sumerians: Their History, Culture, and Character. University of Chicago Press. Rev. Edition. Chicago. 1978

325-Y Aharoni. Lachish V. The Sanctuary and Residency. Institute of Archaeology. Tel Aviv. 1975

326-F. I Andersen, and D. N. Freedman. Hosea. Garden City, Doubleday. New York. 1980

327- Oliver J. Thatcher, editor. The Library of Original Sources, Vol. III. University Research Extension Co., Milwaukee. 1901

328-Cuneiform Inscriptions of Western Asia, Vol. I, plates 17 to 27. Professor Oppert. London 1865-66

329-Histoire des Empires de Chaldée et d'Assyrie: Extrait des Annales de Philosophie Chrétienne, tome. IX, London, Paris, 1865

330-The Texts of the Ugaritic Data Bank. Jesús-Luis Cunchillos, Juan-Pablo Vita and José-Ángel Zamora, Gorgias Press, 2005

331-The Ugaritic Textbook, Revised Edition. Cyrus Gordon. Gorgias Press, Rev. Ed. 1998

332-Mitchell Dahood. Ugaritic-Hebrew Philology. 1965

333-Ernest R. Martinez, S.J. Hebrew-Ugaritic Index to the Writings of Mitchell J. Dahood, volumes I and II. 1981

334- Stan Rummel and Loren Fisher. The Ras Shamra Parallels, volumes I, II and III. 1981

335-Henri Masse. Persian Beliefs and Customs. HRAF New Haven. 1954

336-Cyrus H. Gordon & Gary A. Rendsburg. The Bible and the Ancient Near East. W. W. Norton & Company. New York & London. 1997

337- G. Ernest Wright & David Noel Freedman. Editors. William Foxwell Albright. What Were the Cherubim? The Biblical Archaeologist Reader. Quadrangle Books. Chicago. 1961

338-Norman Cohn. Cosmos, Chaos, and the World to Come, The Ancient Roots of Apocalyptic Faith. Yale University Press. New Haven and London. 1993

339-B. W. Anderson. Names of God. Vol. 2. The Interpreter's Dictionary of the Bible. Abingdon Press. Nashville 1962

340-Barry J. Beitzel. Exodus 3:14 and the Divine Name: A Case of Biblical Paronomasia. Trinity Journal. Trinity Evangelical Divinity School. 1980

341-Albert T. Clay. The Empire of the Amorites. Yale University Press. New Haven. 1919

342-Albert. T. Clay. The Origin of Biblical Traditions: Hebrew Legends in Babylonia and Israel. Yale University Press. New Haven. 1923

343-A. Finet. Iawa-ila, roi de Talhayum. Revue de Syria. Vol. 41. 1964

344-T. H. Gaster. G.A. Buttrick, Editor. Myth, Mythology. The Interpreter's Dictionary of the Bible. Abingdon Press. Nashville, Tennessee. 1962

345-John Gray. Near Eastern Mythology, Mesopotamia, Syria and Palestine. London. Hamlyn. 1969

346-J. C. L. Gibson. Canaanite Myths and Legends.. T&T Clark Ltd. Edinburgh, Scotland. 1978

347-Alexander Heidel. The Gilgamesh Epic and Old Testament Parallels. University of Chicago Press. Chicago. 1946

348-Alexander Heidel. The Babylonian Genesis, The Story of Creation. University of Chicago Press. Chicago. 1942

349-James K. Hoffmeier. The Origins of Israel's God. Ancient Israel in Sinai, The Evidence for the Authenticity of the Wilderness Tradition. Oxford University Press. Oxford & New York. 2005

350-Herbert B. Huffmon. Amorite Personal Names in the Mari Texts: A Structural and Lexical Study. The Johns Hopkins Press. Baltimore, Maryland. 1965

351-Herbert B. Huffmon. Yahweh and Mari. Hans Goedicke. Editor. Near Eastern Studies in Honor of William Foxwell Albright. Johns Hopkins University Press. Baltimore, Maryland. 1971

352-J. Philip Hyatt. Exodus. Marshall, Morgan & Scott. London. 1971

353-19-Samuel Noah Kramer. Sumerian Mythology: A Study of Spiritual and Literary Achievement in the Third Millennium B.C.. University of Pennsylvania Press. Philadelphia. Reprint. 1997

354-Gwendolyn Leick. A Dictionary of Ancient Near Eastern Mythology. Routledge. London & New York. Reprint. 1991

355-Stephen Herbert Langdon. The Mythology of All Races-Semitic. Vol. 5. Marshall Jones Company. Boston. 1931

356-Theophilus G. Pinches. The Old Testament in the Light of the Historical Records and Legends of Assyria and Babylonia. The Society For Promoting Christian Knowledge. London. 1908

357-James B. Pritchard. Editor. The Ancient Near East, An Anthology of Texts and Pictures. Princeton University Press. 1958

358-John William Rogerson. Genesis 1-11. Journal for the Study of the Old Testament. University of Sheffield. Sheffield. 1991.

359-Nahum M. Sarna. Understanding Genesis. Shocken Books. New York. 1966. Reprint. 1970.

360-Henry O. Thompson. David Noel Freedman. Editor. Yahweh. Vol. 6. Anchor Bible Dictionary. Doubleday. New York. 1992

361-Micheal Avi-Yonah & Ephraim Stern, Editors. Encyclopedia of Archaeological Excavations in the Holy Land. Englewood Cliffs, Prentice-Hall. New Jersey. 1975

362-Israel Finkelstein & Neil Asher Silberman. The Bible Unearthed, Archaeology's New Vision of Ancient Israel and the Origin of Its Sacred Texts. The Free Press. New York. 2001

363-Burton MacDonald. East of the Jordan, Territories and Sites of the Hebrew Scriptures. Boston. American Schools of Oriental Research. 2000

364-Avraham Negev, Editor. Archaeological Encyclopedia of the Holy Land. The Jerusalem Publishing House. Jerusalem. 1972.

365-Ephraim Stern. Archaeology of the Land of the Bible, The Assyrian, Babylonian and Persian Periods. Vol.2. Doubleday. New York. 2001

366-W.F. Albright. The Archaeology of Palestine. Harmondsworth. Cambridge. 1991.

367-Y. Aharoni. Archaeology of the land of Israel: From the prehistoric beginnings to the end of the First Temple period. Westminister Press. Philadelphia. 1982.

368-Y. Aharoni. New Aspects of the Israelite Occupation in the North," Near Eastern Archaeology in the Twentieth Century, Essays in Honor of Nelson Gleuck. New York. 1970

369-A. Ben-Tor. Archaeology of Ancient Israel. Yale University Press. New Haven. 1992

370- J.F. Brug. Literary and archaeological study of the Philistines. B.A.R. Oxford. 1985

371-Trude Dothan. People of the Sea: The Search for the Philistines. MacMillan. New York. 1992

372-T. Dothan. Philistines and their material culture. Yale University Press. New Haven. 1982

373- R. Drews. The End of the Bronze Age. Princeton University Press. Princeton. 1993

374- J.F. Drinkard. Benchmarks in time and culture: An introduction to the history and methodology of Syro-Palestinian archaeology. Scholars Press. Atlanta. 1988

375- Israel Finkelstein. The Archaeology of the Israelite Settlement. Jerusalem. 1988

376-Israel Finkelstein, and N. Na'aam. From Nomadism to Monarchy: Archaeological and historical aspects of early Israel. Biblical Archaeology Society. Jerusalem. 1994

377- B. Halpern. The Emergence of Israel in Canaan. Scholars Press. California. 1983

378-T.Levy. The Archaeology of Society in the Holy Land. Facts on File, Inc. New York. 1995

379-A. Kempinski. Rise of an urban culture: the urbanization of Palestine in the Early Bronze Age: Israel Ethnographic Society. Jerusalem. 1978

380-K. Kenyon. Amorites and Canaanites. Oxford University Press. London. 1966

381- K.A. Kenyon. Archaeology in the Holy Land. E. Benn. London. 1979

382- H.D. Lance. The Old Testament and the Archaeologist. Fortress Press. Philadelphia. 1981

383-A. Mazar. Archaeology of the Land of the Bible. Doubleday. New York. 1990

384- M. Magnusson, Archaeology of the Bible. Simon & Schuster. New York. 1978

385- P.R.S. Moorey. A Century of Biblical Archaeology. Cambridge. 1991

386-P.R.S. Moorey. The Bible and Recent Archaeology. London. 1989

387-P.L. Niels. Canaanites and their land: the tradition of the Canaanites. JSOT Press. Sheffield. 1991

388- J.B. Pritchard. Atlas of the Bible. Harpers Collins. London. 1987

389-D.B. Reford. Egypt, Canaan and Israel in Ancient Times. Princeton University Press. Princeton. 1992

390- M. Roaf. Cultural Atlas of Ancient Mesopotamia and the Ancient Near East. Equinox. Oxford. 1990

391-J. Rogerson, Atlas of the Bible. Oxford. 1989

392-W.S. Smith. The Art and Architecture of Ancient Egypt. Yale University Press. New Haven. 1981

393-W.A. Ward, and M. Joukowsky. The Crisis Years: the 12th Century B.C. Kendall/Hunt. Dubuque. 1992

394-Manfred Weippert. The Settlement of the Israelite Tribes in Palestine. Illinois. 1971

395-Ulan Bator. Mongyol-yin uran joqijal (Mongolian literature). 1987

396-Mandaqu. Mongyol Ulus-yin Keblel-yin rajar. 1981

397-Mongyol domoy-yin ufir (On Mongol myth). Mongyol kele utqa joqijal. Mongolian Institute of Language and Literature. 1963

398-Ulema Sadqi. Kira'at Al Fik'r. Cairo. 1960

399-Ulema: Kitab Rama-Doushi, Cairo, Rev. Edition. 1210

400-Ulema Bakri: Dirasat Chams Al Maeeref Al Koubra. Cairo. 1946

401-Ulema Suleiman Bin Al Mahdi. Dirasat fi Woujoud Al Insan. Damascus. 1760

402-John Bowker. The Tarums & Rabbinic Literature. Cambridge University Press. Cambridge. 1969
403-Jacob Neusner. Genesis Rabbah. Scholars Press. 1985
404-Ilil Arbel. Maimonides: A Spiritual Biography. Crossroad Publishing Company. New York. 2001
405-Sabatino Moscati. The face of the Ancient Orient: A Panorama of Near Eastern Civizations in Pre-Classical Times. Quadrangle Books. 1960
406- Georges Roux, La Mésopotamie. Seuil, collection Points histoire. Paris. 1995
407-Rosalie David and Anthony E. David. A Biographical Dictionary of Ancient Egypt. Seaby. 1992
408-Winli & Sadqi: Dirasat and Rouya; Readings, Kuala Lumpuur. 1951
409-Ainsworth W. Travels and researches in Asia Minor, Mesopotamia, Chaldea and Armenia. London.1842
500-Akurgal Ekrem. Ancient Civilizations and Ruins of Turkey. Istanbul. 1969
410-Bieber Margaret. The History of the Greek and Roman Theater. Princeton. 1971
411-Boase T.S.R. The Cilician Kingdom of Armenia. Edinburgh 1978
412-Richard A. Gabriel.The Great Armies of Antiquity. Praeger. 2002
413-Black, J.A., Cunningham, G., Robson, E., and Zólyomi, G., The Electronic Text Corpus of Sumerian Literature. Oxford. 1998
414-Benjamin Foster. From distant days: Myths, tales and poetry from Ancient Mesopotamia. CDI Press. Bethesda. 1995
415-Gwendolyn Leick. A Dictionary of Near Eastern Mythology. Routledge. London. 1991.
416- François Vallat. The most ancient scripts of Iran: The current situation. World Archaeology, vol 17. 1986
417- C. B. F. Walker. Cuneiform: Reading the Past: Ancient Writing from Cuneiform to the Alphabet, first edition, University of California Press. Berkeley. 1990
418-Florian Coulmas. The Blackwell Encyclopedia of Writing Systems. Blackwell Publisher. Oxford. 1996.

419- Jean Bottéro, and Samuel Noah Kramer. Lorsque les dieux faisaient l'homme. (revised edition), Éditions Gallimard. Paris. 1993

420-Fadhil A Ali. Sumerian Letters: Two Collections from the Old Babylonian Schools. University of Pennsylvania. Philadelphia. 1964

421-Herman L. J. Vanstiphout. Joins Proposed in Sumerian Literary Compositions. NABU. 1987

422-Veronika Afanas'eva. Das sumerische Sargon-Epos. Versuch einer Interpretation. Altorientalische Forschungen. 1987

423-Abdul-Hadi, Al-Fouadi. Enki's Journey to Nippur: The Journeys of the Gods. University of Pennsylvania, Philadelphia. 1969.

424-H. Limet. Le poème épique 'Inanna et Ebih'. Une version des lignes 123 à 182. Orientalia . Paris. 1971

425-Dumuzi's dream. Aspects of oral poetry in a Sumerian myth. (Mesopotamia. Copenhagen Studies in Assyriology 1). Akademisk Forlag. Copenhagen. 1972

426-The Instructions of Suruppak. (Mesopotamia. Copenhagen Studies in Assyriology 10). Akademisk Forlag. Copenhagen. 1974

427-On the Earliest Sumerian Literary Tradition. Journal of Cuneiform Studies 28. 1976

428-Geshtinanna as Singer and the Chorus of Uruk and Zabalam: UET 6/1 22. Journal of Cuneiform Studies 37. 1985

429-The Uriah Letter in the Sumerian Sargon Legend. Zeitschrift für Assyriologie 77. Berlin. 1987

430-Marriage and Love in the Sumerian Love Songs. M.E Cohen, D.C. Snell, and D. B. Weisberg. CDL. Bethesda, Maryland. 1993

431-Inez Bernhardt, and S. N Kramer. Götter-Hymnen und Kult-Gesänge der Sumerer auf zwei Keilschrift-"Katalogen" in der Hilprecht-Sammlung." Wissenschaftliche Zeitschrift der Friedrich-Schiller-Universität Jena 6. 1956

432-William W Hallo. Sumerian Canonical Compositions. Individual Focus: The Context of Scripture. Canonical Compositions from the Biblical World. Leiden, Köln. Brill. New York. 1997

433-Hermann Behrens. Loding. T. Darlene, Martha Roth, Alster, Bendt and Walker. "Some literary texts in the British Museum: DUMU-E$_2$-DUB-BA-A. Studies in honor of Åke W. Sjöberg. Publications of the Samuel Noah Kramer Fund. University Museum. Philadelphia. 1989

434 Eléments de linguistique sumérienne. Orbis Biblicus et Orientalis Sonderband. Fribourg/Göttingen: Editions Universitaires/Vandenhoeck & Ruprecht. Paris. 1993

435-A. Barnstone and W. Barnstone. A Book of Women Poets from Antiquity to Now. Schocken. New York. 1980

436-J. Bauer. Zeitschrift der deutschen Morgenländischen Gesellschaft. Berlin. 1977

437-Erle Leichty, Maria de J Ellis, Pamela Gerardi, Hermann Behrens. Enlil und Ninlil. Ein sumerischer Mythos aus Nippur. Studia Pohl Series Major 8. Biblical Institute Press. Rome. 1978

438-Eine Axt für Nergal. A Scientific Humanist Studies in Memory of Abraham Sachs. The University Museum. Philadelphia 1988

439-Franz Steiner Verlag. Die Ninegalla-Hymne. Die Wohnungnahme Inannas in Nippur in altbabylonischer Zeit. (Freiburger altorientalische Studien 21). Stuttgart. 1998

440-Like a Clod thrown into Water: On the translation of a Sumerian Proverbial phrase." Wiener Zeitschrift für die Kunde des Morgenlandes 86. Berlin. 1996

441-J. A Black, M.E Vogelzang, and H.L.J Vanstiphout. Some structural features of Sumerian narrative poetry in Mesopotamian Epic Literature. The Edwin Mellen Press. Lewiston/Queenston/Lampeter.1992

442-Reading Sumerian poetry. Athlone Publications in Egyptology and Ancient Near Eastern Studies. Athlone. London. 1998

443-Borger, Rykle, Hinz,Walther, Römer, H. Willem. Historisch-chronologische Texte, I. Kaiser, Otto, ed. (Texte aus der Umwelt des Alten Testaments I, 4). Gütersloh: Gütersloher Verlagshaus Gerd Mohn. Berlin. 1984

444- Bottéro, J. "La "tenson" et la réflexion sur les choses en Mésopotamie." Pp. 7-22 in Dispute Poems and Dialogues in the Ancient and Medieval Near East. Reinink, G. and Vanstiphout,

Herman L.J., eds. (Orientalia Lovaniensia Analecta 42). Leuven: Peeters, 1991.

445- Françoise Bruschweiler. Inanna: la déesse triomphante et vaincue dans la cosmologie sumérienne. Recherche lexicographique. (Les cahiers du CEPOA 4). Leuven: Éditions Peeters. 1987

446-A. Cavigneaux, and F.N.H. Al-Rawi, Gilgamesh et Taureau de Ciel (shul-mè-kam) (Textes de Tell Haddad IV). Revue d'Assyriologie. Paris. 1993

447-Gilgamesh et la Mort. Texts de Tell Haddad VI, avec un appendice sur les textes funéraires sumériens. (Cuneiform Monographs, 19). Groningen: Styx Publications. Paris. 2000

448-La fin de Gilgamesh, Enkidu et les Enfres d'après les manuscrits d'Ur et de Meturan (Textes de Tell Haddad VIII). Iraq. Paris. 2000

449- J. Stephen Lieberman. Lexicography in Sumerological studies. University of Chicago Press. Chicago. 1974

450-D. Charpin. Le Clergé d'Ur au siècle d'Hammurapi. Bibliothèque des histories. Gallimard/NRF. Paris. 1986

451-The Message of Lú-dingir-ra to His Mother'and a Group of Akkado-Hittite 'Proverbs. Journal of Near Eastern Studies. 1964

452-A. Leo Oppenheim. Hymn to the Beer Goddess and a Drinking Song. The Oriental Institute of the University of Chicago. Chicago. 1964

453 -ean-Marie Durand, and Jean-Robert Kupper. Sur les livres d'écolier à l'époque paléo-babylonienne. Mélanges offerts a Maurice Birot. Éditions Recherche sur les Civilisations. Paris. 1985

454-William W. Hallo, Marc E Cohen, Snell, C.Daniel, David Weisberg. On Mesopotamian Jails and Their Lady Warden. CDL Press. Bethesda. Maryland. 1993

455-Marc E Cohen. The Incantation-Hymn: Incantation or Hymn? Journal of the American Oriental Society. 1975

456-Mark E. Cohen, Snell, D.C. and Weisberg. The Tablet and the Scroll. CDL Press. Bethesda. Maryland. 1993

457- Jerrold S Cooper. New Cuneiform Parallels to the Song of Songs. Journal of Biblical Literature. 1971

458-The Return of Ninurta to Nippur. (Analecta Orientalia). Rome: Pontificium Institutum Biblicum, 1978
459-Kort, Ann and Morschauser, Scott, eds. Sargon and Jospeh: Dreams Come True. Biblical and Related Studies Presented to Samuel Iwry.. Eisenbrauns. Winona Lake, Indiana, 1985
460- Cooper, J.S. and Heimpel, W. "The Sumerian Sargon Legend." Journal of the American Oriental Society 103. 1983
461- Çig, Muazzez, Kizilyay, Hatice and Kramer, Samuel Noah. Istanbul Sümer Edebî Tablet ve Parçalari. 1976.
462-Deimel, A. Shumerische Grammatik mit Übungsstücken und zwei Anhängen. Rome: Pontifical Biblical Institute, 1939.
463-Dupret, Marie-Astrid. Hymne au dieu Numushda avec prière en faveur de Sîniqisham de Larsa. Orientalia 43. 1974
464- J.-M Durand. Sumerica. Revue d'Assyriologie 84. 1990
465- Edzard, Dietz Otto. Die Zweite Zwischenzeit Babyloniens.. Otto Harrassowitz. Wiesbaden 1957
466-Enmebaragesi von Kish. Zeitschrift für Assyriologie 53. 1969
467-Gudea and His Dynasty. (The Royal Inscriptions of Mesopotamia. Early Periods 3, 1). University of Toronto Press. Toronto/Buffalo/London. 1997
468- Gilgamesh und Huwawa. Zwei Versionen der sumerischen Zedernwaldepisode nebst einer Edition von Version B. Sitzungberichte der Bayerischen Akademie der Wissenschaften. Philosophisch-historische Klasse. 1993
469- Edzard, D.O. and Wilcke, Cl. Die Hendursanga-Hymne. Kramer Anniversary Volume. Cuneiform Studies in honor of Samuel Noah Kramer. Eichler, Barry L., Heimerdinger, Jane W. and Sjöberg, Åke W., eds. (Alter Orient und Altes Testament 25). Neukirchen-Vluyn: Butzon & Bercker Kevelaer. 1976
470-Quasi-Duplikate zur 'Hendursanga-Hymne. Archiv für Orientforschung 25. 1974
471-Falkenstein, A. Untersuchungen zur sumerischen Grammatik (Forsetzung). Zeitschrift für Assyriologie. 1944
472-Ein sumerisches Kultlied auf Samsu'iluna. Archiv Orientální. 1949
473-Sumerische religiöse Texte. Zeitschrift für Assyriologie. 1950

474-Das Potentialis- und Irrealissufix -e-she des Sumerischen. Indogermanische Forschungen 60. 1952

475-Sumerische Hymnen und Gebete. Sumerische und akkadische Hymnen und Gebete. Falkenstein, Adam and von Soden, Wolfram, eds. Zürich/Stuttgart. Artemis, 1953

476-Tammuz. Rencontre Assyriologique Internationale 3. (Comptes rendus des Rencontres Assyriologiques Internationales 3). Leiden. 1954

477-Sumerische Götterlieder. (Abhandlungen der Heidelberger Akademie der Wissenschaften, Phil.-hist. Kl., Jahrgang 1959, 1. Abh.) Heidelberg. Carl Winter UniversitätsVerlag, 1959

478-Farber-Flüge, Gertrud. Der Mythos Inanna und Enki unter besonderer Berücksichtigung der Liste der me. (Studia Pohl 10). Biblical Institute Press. Rome. 1973

479-Zur sogenannten Samsuilunahymne PBS 10/2 Nr. 11. Eichler, Barry L., Heimerdinger, Jane W. and Sjöberg, Åke W., eds. (Alter Orient und Altes Testament 25). Neukirchen-Vluyn. Butzon & Bercker Kevelaer. 1976

480-Farber, Gertrud. "Inanna and Enki, a Sumerian Myth Revisited. Journal of Near Eastern Studies . 1995

481- Sumerian Canonical Compositions. Myths: Inanna and Enki (1.161) The Context of Scripture, I: Canonical Compositions from the Biblical World. Hallo, William W., ed. Leiden/New York/Köln. Brill. 1997

482-Ferrara, A.J. Nanna-Suen's Journey to Nippur. (Studia Pohl Series Major 2) Biblical Institute Press, Rome . 1973

483-Finkelstein, J.J. The Antediluvian Kings: A University of California Tablet. Journal of Cuneiform Studies. 1963

484-Urnamma of Ur in Sumerian Literary Tradition. (Orbis Biblicus et Orientalis). Fribourg, Switzerland /Göttingen University Press /Vandenhoeck & Ruprecht. 1999

485-Karen Focke."Die Göttin Nin-imma. Zeitschrift für Assyriologie. 1998

486-Old Babylonian Period (2003-1595 BC). (The Royal Inscriptions of Mesopotamia. Early Periods 4). Toronto/Buffalo/London: University of Toronto Press. 1990

487-Sargonic and Gutian Periods (2334-2113 BC). (The Royal Inscriptions of Mesopotamia. Early Periods 2). Toronto/Buffalo/London: University of Toronto Press, 1993

488- Frayne, Douglas and George, Lynne. "The "Rakes's" Progress: A Phantom King of Kish." NABU (1990

489- George, Andrew. The Epic of Gilgamesh. The Babylonian Epic Poem and Other Texts in Akkadian and Sumerian. Harmondsworth, Middlesex: Allen Lane The Penguin Press, 1999

490- Goedicke, H. and Roberts, J.J.H., eds. Unity and Diversity: Essays in the History, Literature and Religion of the Ancient Near East. (The Johns Hopkins Near Eastern Studies 7). Baltimore/London, 1975

491- Gragg, Gene B. "The Kesh Temple Hymn." Pp. 155-189 in The Collection of the Sumerian Temple Hymns. Sjöberg, Åke W., Bergmann, E. and Gragg, Gene B., eds. (Texts from Cuneiform Sources III). Locust Valley, New York: J.J. Augustin, 1969

492- Sumerian Dimensional Infixes. (Alter Orient und Altes Testament Sonderreihe 5). Kevelaer/Neukirchen-Vluyn: Butzon & Bercker/Neukirchener, 1973

493- Groneberg, Brigitte R.M. Lob der Ishtar. Gebet un Ritual and die altbabylonische Venusgöttin. Tanatti Ishtar. (Cuneiform Monographs 8). Groningen: Styx Publications, 1997

494-Gurney, O.R. and Kramer, S.N. Sumerian Literary Texts in the Ashmolean Museum. (Oxford Editions of Cuneiform Texts 5). Oxford: Oxford University Press, 1976

495- Hallo, William W. "Beginning and End of the Sumerian King List in the Nippur Recension." Journal of Cuneiform Studies 17 (1963

496- The Cultic Setting of Sumerian Poetry." Pp. 117-134 in Actes de la XVIIe Rencontre Assyriologique Internationale. Université Libre de Bruxelles 30 Juin-4 Juillet 1969. Finet, André, ed. (Publications de Comité belge de recherches historiques, épigraphiques et archéologiques en Mésopotamie 1). Ham-sur-Heure: Comité belge de recherches en Mésopotamie, 1970

497- The Birth of Kings. Love and Death in the Ancient Near East: Essays in Honor of Marvin H. Pope. Marks, J.H. and Good, R.M., eds. Four Quarters Publishing Company: Guilford, 1987

498-Sumerian Canonical Compositions. A. Divine Focus. 2. Hymns: The Blessing of Nisaba by Enki (1.1.63) (NIN-MUL-AN-GIM). The Context of Scripture, I: Canonical Compositions from the Biblical World. Hallo, William W., ed. Leiden/New York/Köln: Brill, 1997

499- Hallo, William W. and van Dijk, J.J.A. The Exaltation of Inanna. (Yale Near Eastern Researches 3). New Haven/London: Yale University Press, 1968

500- Heimerdinger, Jane W. Sumerian literary fragments from Nippur. (Occasional Publications of the Babylonian Fund 4). Philadelphia, Pa.: The University Museum, Philadelphia, 1979

501- Heimpel, W. Tierbilder in der sumerischen Literatur. (Studia Pohl, series minor 2). Rome: Pontifical Biblical Institute, 1968

502-Hrushka, Blahoslav. "Das Verhältnis zur Vergangheit im alten Mesopotamien." Archív Orientálni 47 (1979

503- Hurowitz, Victor (Avigdor). "Building stories in Sumerian and Old Babylonian Literature. I Have Built You an Exalted House. Temple Building in the Bible in Light of Mesopotamian and Northwest Semitic Writings. (JSOT Supplement Series 115). Sheffield, 1992

504-Primitive Democracy in Ancient Mesopotamia. Toward the Image of Tammuz and Other Essays on Mesopotamian History and Culture. Moran, W.L., ed. Harvard University Press. Cambridge. Mass. 1970

505-Early Political Development in Mesopotamia: Toward the Image of Tammuz and Other Essays on Mesopotamian History and Culture. Moran, W. L., ed. Cambridge, Mass., Harvard University Press. 1970

506- Religious Drama in Ancient Mesopotamia. Unity and Diversity: Essays in the History, Literature and Religion of the Ancient Near East. Goedicke, H. and Roberts, J.J.H., eds. (The Johns Hopkins Near Eastern Studies 7). Baltimore/London. 1976

507-Death in Mesopotamia (Abstract). Death in Mesopotamia. Papers Read at the XXVIe Rencontre assyriologique internationale. Alster, Bendt, ed. (Mesopotamia 8). Copenhagen: Akademisk Forlag, 1980

508-Two bal-bal-e Dialogues. Love and Death in the Ancien Near East: Essays in Honor of Marvin H. Pope. Marks, J.H. and Good, R.M., eds. Guilford: Four Quarters Publishing Company. 1987

509-M. Fishbane and E. Tov. The Spell of Nudimmud. Sha'arei Talmon: Studies Presented to Shemarjahu Talmon. Eisenbrauns. Winona Lake, Indiana. 1992

510- Ilmari Kärki. Die Königsinschriften der Dritten Dynastie von Ur. (Studia Orientalia 58). Finnish Oriental Society. Helsinki. 1986

511-Katz, Diana. "Gilgames and Akka: Was Uruk Ruled by Two Assembles?" Revue d'Assyriologie et d'Archeologie orientale. 1987

512-A.D. Kilmer. J. Bankier and D. Lashgari. Women Poets of the World. Macmillan. New York. 1983

513- Klein, Jacob. "Shulgi and Gilgamesh: Two Brother-Peers (Shulgi O). Kramer Anniversary Volume. Cuneiform Studies in Honor of Samuel Noah Kramer. Eichler, Barry L., Heimerdinger, Jane W. and Sjöberg, Åke W., eds. (Alter Orient und Altes Testament 25). Neukirchen-Vluyn: Butzon & Bercker Kevelaer. 1976

514- The Royal Hymns of Shulgi King of Ur: Man's Quest for Immortal Fame. (Transactions of the American Philosophical Society 71, VII). The American Philosophical Society. Philadelphia. 1981

515- Three Shulgi Hymns. Sumerian Royal Hymns Gloryfying King Shulgi of Ur. Ramat-Gan: Bar Ilan University Press. 1981

516- 'Personal God' and Individual Prayer in Sumerian Religion. Archiv für Orientforschung Beiheft 19. 1982

517- The Capture of Akka by Gilgamesh (GA 81 and 99). Journal of the American Oriental Society 103. 1983

518- The Birth of a Crownprince in the Temple: A Neo-Sumerian Literary Topos. La femme dans le Proche-Orient Antique. RAI 33. Durand, J.-M., ed. Paris: Editions Recherche sur les Civilisations.1987

519-Shulgi and Ishmedagan: Originality and Dependency in Sumerian Royal Hymnology. Bar-Ilan Studies in Assyriology Dedicated to Pinhas Artzi. Klein, Jacob and Skaist, Aaron, eds.

(Bar-Ilan Studies in Near Eastern Languages and Culture). Ramat-Gan: Bar-Ilan University Press. 1990

520-A New Nippur Duplicate of the Sumerian Kinglist in the Brockmon Collection, University of Haifa. Velles Paraules. Ancient Near Eastern Studies in Honor of Miguel Civil on the Occasion of his Sixty-Fifth Birthday. Michalowski, P., Steinkeller, P., Stone, E. C. and Zettler, R.L., eds. (Aula Orientalis 9). Sabadell. Editorial Ausa. Barcelona 1991

521-The Coronation and Consecration of Shulgi in the Ekur (Shulgi G) Ah, Assyria. Studies in Assyrian History and Ancient Near eastern Historiography Presented to Hayim Tadmor. Cogan, M. and Eph'al, I., eds. (Scripta Hierosolymitana 33). The Magnes Press. Jerusalem. 1991

522-A.F. Rainey. The Marriage of Martu.kinattutu sha darâti. Raphael Kutscher Memorial Volume. Aviv University. Institute of Archaeology. Tel Aviv. 1993

523-The God Martu in Sumerian Literature. Sumerian Gods and Their Representation. Finkel, I.L. and Geller, Mark J., eds. (Cuneiform Monographs 7). Styx Publications. Groningen. 1997

524- Sumerian Canonical Compositions. A. Divine Focus. 4. Lamentations: Lamentation over the Destruction of Sumer and Ur (1.166). The Context of Scripture, I: Canonical Compositions from the Biblical World. Hallo, William W., ed. Leiden/New York/Köln. Brill. 1997

525- The Sweet Chant of the Churn: A revised edition of Ishmedagan J. dubsar anta-men. Studien zur Altorientalisk. Festschrift für Willem H.Ph. Römer. (Alter Orient Und Altes Testament 253). Ugarit-Verlag. Münster. 1998

526-Koefoed, Aase. Gilgames, Enkidu and the Nether World. Acta Sumerologica 5. 1983

527- Géza Komoróczy. Lobpreis auf das Gefängnis in Sumer. Acta Antiqua Academiae Scientiarum Hungaricae . 1975

528- Samuel Noah Kramer. Lamentation Over the Destruction of Ur. (Assyriological Studies 12). Chicago University Press. Chicago. 1940

529-Sumerian Literary Texts from Nippur in the Museum of the Ancient Orient at Istanbul. (The Annual of the American Schools of Oriental Research). New Haven: The American Schools of Oriental Research. 1944

530- Man and His God: A Sumerian Variation on the Job Motif." Wisdom in Israel and in the Ancient Near East Presented to Professor Harold Henry Rowley. Noth, M. and Thomas, D. W., eds. (Supplements to Vetus Testamentum 3). Leiden. Brill. 1955

531-Corrections and additions to SRT." Zeitschrift für Assyriologie 52. 1957

532-Hymn to the Ekur." Pp. 95-102 in Scritti in onore di Giuseppe Furlani. (Rivista degli Studi Orientali 32). Roma. Giovanni Bardi, 1957.

533-Two Elegies on a Pushkin Museum Tablet: A New Sumerian Literary Genre. Oriental Literature Publishing House, Moscow. 1960.

534-Kataloge." Pp. 19-20 in Sumerische literarische Texte aus Nippur. Kramer, Samuel Noah and Bernhardt, Ines, eds. (Texte und Materialien der Frau Professor Hilprecht-Sammlung Jena NF 3). 1961.

535-The Sumerians. The University of Chicago Press. Chicago. 1963.

536-Cuneiform Studies and the History of Literature: The Sumerian Sacred Marriage Texts. Proceedings of the American Philosophical Society . 1963

537-The Death of Ur-Nammu and His descent to the Netherworld. Journal of Cuneiform Studies 21. 1967

538 James B Pritchard. Sumerian Hymns.Ancient Near Eastern Texts Relating to the Old Testament. Princeton University Press. Princeton. 1969

539-James B Pritchard. Sumerian Lamentation.Ancient Near Eastern Texts Relating to the Old Testament. Princeton University Press. Princeton. 1969

540- James B Pritchard. Sumerian Wisdom Text. Ancient Near Eastern Texts Relating to the Old Testament. Princeton University Press. Princeton 1969

541-The Sacred Marriage Rite: Aspects of Faith, Myth, and Ritual in Ancient Sumer. Indiana University Press. Bloomington. 1969

542-James B Pritchard. Sumerian Miscellaneous Texts. Ancient Near Eastern Texts Relating to the Old Testament. Princeton University Press. Princeton. 1969

543-u_5-a a-u_5-a: A Sumerian Lullaby (with Appendix by Thorkild Jacobsen). Studi in onore di Edoardo Volterra. Milano: Università di Roma. 1971

544-The Jolly Brother: A Sumerian Dumuzi Tale. Journal Of Ancient Near Eastern Studies 5. 1973

545-Two British Museum irshemma. Studia Orientalia. London. 1975

546-The Ur excavations and Sumerian literature. University of Chigaco Expedition. 1977

547-Sumerian literature and the British Museum: the promise of the future. Proceedings of the American Philosophical Society. 1980

548-Ruth Adler, Milton Arfa, Gary Rendsburg, and Nathan T. Winter. Inanna and the numun-plant: A new Sumerian myth. KTAV Publishing House/The Institute of Hebrew Culture and Education of New York University. New York. 1980

549-The Sumerian Deluge Myth. Reviewed and Revised. Anatolian Studies 33. 1983

550-Ninurta's Pride and Punishment. Aula Orientalis 2.1984

551- Bread for Enlil, Sex for Inanna. Orientalia 54. 1985

552-The Churn's Sweet Sound: A Sumerian Bucolic Poem. Eretz-Israel 20. 1989

553-BM 100042: A Hymn to Shu-Sin and an Adab of Nergal." Pp. 303-316 in DUMU-E₂-DUB-BA-A. Studies in Honor of Åke W. Sjöberg. Behrens, Hermann, Loding, Darlene and Roth, Martha T., eds. (Occasional Publications of the Samuel Noah Kramer Fund 11). Philadelphia: The University Museum, Philadelphia. 1989

554-The Marriage of Martu." Pp. 11-27 in Bar-Ilan Studies in Assyriology Dedicated to Pinhas Artzi. Klein, Jacob and Skaist, Aaron, eds. Ramat Gan: Bar-Ilan University Press. 1990

555-The Barnett Enmerkar Tablet: a New Sumerian Dialect De la Babylonie à la Syrie, en passant par Mari: Mélanges offerts à Monsieur J.-R. Kupper à l'occasion de son 70e anniversaire. Tunca, O., ed. Liège. 1990

556- Mori, Masao, Ogawa, Hideo and Yoshikawa, Mamoru, The Death of Ur-Nammu. eds. Wiesbaden: Otto Harrassowitz. 1991

557-Kramer, Samuel N. and Bernhardt, Inez. Sumerische Literarische Texte aus Nippur in der Hilprecht Sammlung. Berlin: Akademie-Verlag. 1967

558-Kramer, Samuel Noah and Maier, J. Myths of Enki, the Crafty God. New York/Oxford: Oxford University Press, 1989.

559-Kraus, F.R. "Zur Liste der älteren Könige von Babylonien." Zeitschrift für Assyriologie 50 (1952

560-Kraus, H.-J. Klagelieder (Threni). (Biblischer Kommentar: Altes Testament). Neukirchen-Vluyn: Neukirchener Verlag. 1968

561-Krecher, Joachim. Sumerische Kultlyrik. Wiesbaden: O. Harrassowitz. 1966

562-Review of Alster 1972." Orientalistische Literaturzeitung 73. 1978

563-Krispijn, Th.J.H. "Beiträge zur altorientalischen Musikforschung: 1. Shulgi und die Musik" Akkadica 70. 1990

564-Dierenfabels in het oude Mesopotamië. In Mijn naam is haas. Dierenverhalen in verschillende culturen. Idema, E.L. et al., ed. Baarn. Ambo. 1993

565-Kutscher, Raphael. "Utu Prepares for Judgment. Eichler, Barry L., Heimerdinger, Jane W. and Sjöberg, Ake W., eds. (Alter Orient und Altes Testament). Butzon & Bercker/Neukirchene. 1976.

566-Lafont, Bertrand. Review of Katz, Gilgamesh and Akka. Bibliotheca Orientalis 53. 1996

567-Lambert, W.G. and Millard, A.R. Atra-Hasis: the Babylonian Story of the Flood. Oxford: Clarendon Press. 1969

568-Langdon, Stephen. Babylonian Liturgies. Paris. Librairie Paul Geuthner.1913

569-Limet, H. Le poème épique Inanna et Ebih. Une version des lignes 123 à 182. Orientalia 40. 1971

570-Ludwig, Marie-Christine. Untersuchungen zu den Hymnen des Ishme-Dagan von Isin. (SANTAG 2). Wiesbaden. Harrassowitz. 1990

571-Malamat, A. Kingship and Council in Israel and Sumer. Journal of Near Eastern Studies 22. 1963

572-Marík, Tomásh. Bemerkungen zur formalen und inhaltlichen Interpretation des Gilgamesh un Akka. Archív Orientální 66. 1998

573-Mattingly, G.L. "The Pious Sufferer: Mesopotamia's Traditional Theodicy and Job's Counselors. Lewiston. Mellen. 1990.

574- Piotr Michalowski. Amar-Su'ena and the Historical Tradition. Archon Books. Hamden. Connecticut. 1977.

575-A New Sumerian Catalogue from Nippur. Oriens Antiquus 19. 1980

576-Review of Römer 1980. Bulletin of the School of Oriental and African Studies 45. 1982

577-Observations on a Sumerian Literary Catalogue from Ur." Journal of Cuneiform Studies 36. 1984

578-Sin-iddinam and Ishkur. A Scientific Humanist: Studies in Memory of Abraham Sachs. Leichty, Erle, Ellis, Maria de J. and Gerardi, Pamela, eds. (Occasional Publications of the Samuel Noah Kramer Fund 9). Philadelphia: The University Museum. 1988

579-The Lamentation over the Destruction of Sumer and Ur. (Mesopotamian Civilizations 2). Winona Lake, IN: Eisenbrauns. 1989

580-The Torch and the Censer. The Tablet and the Scroll: Near Eastern Studies in Honor of William W. Hallo. Cohen, Mark E., Snell, Daniel C. and Weisberg, David B., eds. Bethesda Md: CDL Press. 1993

581-Literature as a source of lexical inspiration: some notes on a hymn to the goddess Inana. Jan Braun, Krystyna Lyczkowska, Maciej Popko and Piotr Steinkeller, eds. Warsaw. Agade. 1998

582-Nissen, H.J."Eineneue Version der Sumerischen Königliste. Zeitschrift für Assyriologie 57. 1965

583-Nougayrol, Jean. Textes Suméro-Accadiens des archives et bibliothéques privées d'Ugarit. Ugaritica 5. 1968

584-Owen, David I. Excerpts from an Unknown Hymn to Rim-Sin of Larsa. Kramer Anniversary Volume. Cuneiform Studies in Honor of Samuel Noah Kramer. Eichler, Barry L., Heimerdinger,

Jane W. and Sjöberg, Å.W., eds. (Alter Orient und Altes Testament 25). Neukirchen-Vluyn: Butzon and Bercker, 1976.
585-Pettinato, Giovanni. Das altorientalische Menschenbild und die sumerischen und akkadischen Schöpfungsmythen. Heidelberg. 1971.
586-Il bicameralismo a Sumer: un topos literario assunto a realtà storica. Rendiconti dell'Academia Nazionale dei Lincei Ser. 9, 5. 1994
587-Pomponio, F. Le sventure di Amar-Suena. Studi Epigrafici e Linguistici 7. 1990
588-Daniel David Reisman, Two Neo-Sumerian Royal Hymns.Ph.D. dissertation. University of Pennsylvania. Philadelphia. 1970
589-Ninurta's Journey to Eridu. Journal of Cuneiform Studies 24. 1971
590-Iddin-Dagan's Sacred Marriage Hymn. Journal of Cuneiform Studies 25. 1973
591-Röllig, Wolfgang. Review of Behrens 1978. Zeitschrift der Deutschen Morgenländischen Gesellschaft 131. 1981
592- W.H. Römer. Sumerische 'Königshymnen' der Isin-Zeit. Leiden. Brill. 1965
593-Einige Beobachtungen zur Göttin Nini(n)sina auf Grund von Quellen der Ur III-Zeit und der altbabylonischen Periode. lishan mithurti. Festschrift Wolfram Freiherr von Soden zum 19 VI. 1968 gewidmet von Schülern und Mitarbeitern. Röllig, W. and Dietrich, M., eds. (Altes Orient und Altes Testament 1). Kevelaer / Neukirchen-Vluyn. Verlag Butzon & Bercker/Neukichener Verlag. 1969
594-Königshymnen der Isinzeit und Königsinvestitur. Zeitschrift der Deutschen Morgenländischen Gesellschaft. XVII. Deutscher Orientalistentag Supplement 1/1. 1969
595-Eine sumerische Hymne mit Selbstlob Inannas. Orientalia 38. 1969
596-Review of Hallo and van Dijk 1968. Ugarit-Forschungen 4. 1972
597-Das sumerische Kurzepos "Gilgamesh and Akka". (Alter Orient und Altes Testament 290, I). Neukirchen-Vluyn: Neukirchener Verlag. 1980.

598-Review of Berlin 1979. Bibliotheca Orientalis 38. 1981

599-Zur Siegesinschrift des Königs Utuhegal von Unug (+- 2116-2110 v. Chr.). Orientalia 54. 1985

600-Totenbefragung: Aus Bilgamesh, Enkidu und die Unterwelt, Z. Deutungen der Zukunft in Briefen, Orakeln und Omina. Kaiser, Otto, ed. (Texte aus der Umwelt des Alten Testaments II, 1). Gütersloh: Gütersloher Verlagshaus Gerd Mohn. 1986.

601-Sumerische Hymnen, II. Bibliotheca Orientalis 45. 1988

602-Aus einem Schulstreitsgespräch in sumerischer Sprache. Ugarit Forschungen 20. 1988

603-Miscellanea Sumerologica I: Zur sumerischen Dichtung "Heirat des Gottes Mardu". Ugarit Forschungen 21. 1989

604-Miscellanea Sumerologica II. zum Sog. Gudam-Text. Bibliotheca Orientalis 48. 1991

605-Die Hymnen des Ishme-Dagan von Isin."Orientalia 62. 1993

606-Ein a-da-ab-Lied auf Ningublaga mit Bitten für König Iddindagan von Isin um Hilfe gegen Feinde wie etwa die Mardubeduinen (Sumerische Hymnen III). Ugarit Forschungen 28. 1996

607-Römer, Willem H.Ph. and Edzard, Dietz Otto. Mythen und Epen. Kaiser, Otto, ed. (Texte aus der Umwelt des Alten Testaments). Gütersloh: Gütersloher Verlagshaus Gerd Mohn. 1993

608-Römer, Willem H.Ph. and Hecker, Karl. Lieder und Gebete. Kaiser, Otto, ed. (Texte Aus der Umwelt des Alten Testaments II, 5). Gütersloh: Gütersloher Verlagshaus Gerd Mohn. 1989

609-Römer, Willem H.Ph. and von Soden, Wolfram. Weisheitstexte. Kaiser, Otto, ed. (Texte aus der Umwelt des Alten Testaments III, 1). Gütersloh: Gütersloher Verlagshaus Gerd Mohn. 1990

610-Rosengarten, Yvonne. Trois Aspects de la Pensée Religieuse Sumérienne. Paris. Editions De Boccard. 1971

611-Roth, Martha T. The Slave and the Scoundrel: CBS 10467, A Sumerian Morality Tale" Journal of the American Oriental Society 103. 1983

612-Sallaberger, Walther. Der kultische Kalender der Ur III-Zeit. (Untersuchungen zur Assyriologie und Vorderasiatische Archäologie 7, I-II).

613-Sauren, Herbert. "Der Feldzug Utuhengals von Uruk gegen Tirigan und das Siedlungsgebiet der Gutäer." Revue d'Assyriologie 61. 1967

614-Nammu and Enki. William W. Hallo. Cohen, M.E, Snell, D.C. and Weisberg, D.B., eds. Bethesda, MD: CDL. 1993

615-Sefati, Yitschak. Love Songs in Sumerian Literature: Critical Edition of the Dumuzi-Inanna Songs.Ph.D. dissertation. Ramat-Gan: Bar-Ilan University. 1985

616-An Oath of Chastity in a Sumerian Love Song (STR31) Bar-Ilan Studies in Assyriology Dedicated to Pinhas Artzi. Klein, Jacob and Skaist, A., eds. Ramat-Gan: Bar-Ilan University Press. 1990

617-Sumerian Canonical Compositions. A. Divine Focus. 6. Love Poems: Dumuzi Inanna Songs (1.169).The Context of Scripture, I: Canonical Compositions from the Biblical World. Hallo, William W., ed. Leiden. New York. Köln.Brill. 1997

618-Love songs in Sumerian literature: critical edition of the Dumuzi-Inanna songs. (Bar-Ilan Studies in Near Eastern Languages and Culture. Publications of the Samuel N. Kramer Institute of Assyriology). Ramat-Gan: Bar-Ilan University Press. 1998.

619-Selz, G.J. "Nissaba(k), 'die Herrin der Getreidezuteilungen'. DUMU-E$_2$-DUB-BA-A. Studies in Honor of Åke W. Sjöberg. Behrens, Hermann, Loding, Darlene and Roth, Martha Tobi, eds. (Occasional Publications of the Samuel Noah Kramer Fund 11). Philadelphia University Museum. 1989.

620- Aaron Shaffer. Sumerian Sources of the Tablet XII of the Epic of Gilgamesh.Ph.D. dissertation. University of Pennsylvania. Philadelphia.

621- Aaron Shaffer, and R.J Tournay . L'épopée de Gilgamesh. Paris. 1994

622-Sjöberg, Åke. Der Mondgott Nanna-Suen in der sumerischen Überlieferung. I. Teil: Texte. Stockholm: Almqvist & Wiksell. 1960

623-Ein syllabisch geschriebener Ur-Nammu-Text. Orientalia Suecana 10. 1961

624-K. Drynjeff, Ringgren, H J. Bergman Prayers for King Hammurabi of Babylon. Ex orbe religionum: Studia Geo Widengren oblata. Pars Prior. (Studies in the History of Religions (Supplements to Numen) . Leiden. Brill. 1972

625-Hymns to Meslamtaea, Lugalgirra and Nanna-Suen in Honour of King Ibbisuen (Ibbisîn) of Ur. Orientalia Suecana 19-20. 1970-1971

626-He is a good seed of a dog" and "Engardu, the fool". Journal of Cuneiform Studies 24. 1972

627-Miscellaneous Sumerian hymns." Zeitschrift für Assyriologie 63. 1973

628-Two Prayers for King Samsuiluna of Babylon." Journal of the American Oriental Society 93. 1973

629-A Hymn to the Goddess Sadarnuna." Journal of the American Oriental Society 93. 1973

630-Nungal in the Ekur." Archiv für Orientforschung 24. 1973

631-Hymn to Numushda with a Prayer for King Sîniqisham of Larsa and a Hymn to Ninurta." Orientalia Suecana 22. 1973

632-In-nin shà-gur$_4$-ra: A Hymn to the Goddess Inanna by the en-Priestess Enheduanna." Zeitschrift für Assyriologie 65. 1975

633-Three hymns to the god Ningishzida." Studia Orientalia 46. 1976

634- Barry L. Eichler, Jane W. Heimerdinger, and Åke W Sjöberg. Hymns to Ninurta with Prayers to Shusîn of Ur and Bursîn of Isin. (Alter Orient und Altes Testament 25). Neukirchen-Vluyn. Butzon & Bercker Kevelaer. 1979

635-A blessing of King Urninurta. Essays on the Ancient Near East in Memory of Jacob Joel Finkelstein. Ellis, Maria de Jong, ed. (Memoirs of the Connecticut Academy of Sciences.) Archon Books. Hamden. Connecticut. 1977

636-The ape from the mountain who became king of Isin. The Tablet and the Scroll: Near Eastern Studies in Honor of William W. Hallo. Cohen, M.E., Snell, D.C. and Weisberg, D.B., eds. Bethesda, MD: CDL Press. 993

637-Sumerian Texts and Fragments in the University of Pennsylvania Museum Related to Rulers of Isin. dubsar anta-

men Studien zur Altorientalistik Festschrift für Willem H.Ph. Römer zur Vollendung seines 70. Lebensjahres mit Beiträgen von Freunden, Schülern und Kollegen. Dietrich, Manfried and Loretz, Oswald, eds. (Alter Orient und Altes Testament). Münster. Ugarit-Verlag. 1998

638-Sjöberg, Åke W. and Bergmann, E. "The Collection of the Sumerian Temple Hymns. The Collection of the Sumerian Temple Hymns. Sjöberg, Åke W., Bergmann, E. and Gragg, Gene B., eds. (Texts from Cuneiform Sources III). Locust Valley, New York: J.J. Augustin. 1969

639-Sladek, William R. Inanna's Descent to the Netherworld. Ann Arbor: University Microfilms. 1974

640-Sollberger, Edmond. "The Tummal Inscription." Journal of Cuneiform Studies 16. 1962

641-The Rulers of Lagash." Journal of Cuneiform Studies 21 . 1967

642-Sollberger, Edmond and Kupper, Jean-Robert. Inscriptions royales sumeriennes et akkadiennes. Les Éditions du Cerf. Paris. 1971

643-Steible, Horst. Ein Lied an den Gott Haja mit Bitte für den König Rimsîn von Larsa.Ph.D. dissertation. Freiburg. 1967

644-Rimsîn, mein König. Drei kultische Texte aus Ur mit der Schlussdoxologie d.ri-im-d.sîn lugal-mu. (Freiburger Altorientalische Studien 1). Wiesbaden. Franz Steiner Verlag. 1975

645- G. Steiner. Der reale Kern in den legendären Zahlen von Regierungsjahren der ältesten Herrscher Mesopotamiens. Acta Sumerologica 10. 1988

646-Huwawa und sein Bergland in der sumerischen Tradition. Acta Sumerologica 18. 1996

647-Steinkeller, Piotr. Nanshe and the Birds. Paper for the Jacobsen Symposium. London. 1994

648-Suter, Claudia E. "Gudeas vermeintliche Segnungen des Eninnu." Zeitschrift für Assyriologie 87. 1997

649-Gudea's Temple Building. The Representation of an Early Mesopotamian Ruler in Text and Image. (Cuneiform Monographs 17). Groningen. Styx Publications. 2000

650-Thomsen, Marie-Louise. 'The home of the fish: a new interpretation. Journal of Cuneiform Studies 27 . 1975
651-Thureau-Dangin, F. "Le déesse Nisaba." Revue d'Assyriologie 7 . 1909
652-La fin de la domination gutienne. Revue d'Assyriologie 9. 1912
653-Un double de l'inscription d'Utu-hegal. Revue d'Assyriologie 10. 1913
654-Tinney, Steve."On the poetry for King Ishme-Dagan. Orientalistische Literaturzeitung. 1995
655-The Nippur Lament. (Occasional Publications of the Samuel Noah Kramer Fund 16). Philadelphia: The University Of Pennsylvania Museum. 1996
656-Notes on Sumerian sexual lyric. Journal of Near Eastern Studies 59. 2000
657-Tournay, R.-J. and Shaffer, A. L'épopée de Gilgamesh. Paris. 1994
658-Van Dijk, J A A. Sumerische Götterlieder. (Abhandlungen der Heidelberger Akademie der Wissenschaften, Phil.-hist. Kl., Abh.) Heidelberg. Carl Winter Universitäts.Verlag. 1960
659-Stefan M. Maul. Inanna raubt den grossen Himmel. Ein mythos. Festschrift für Rykle Borger zu seinem 65. Geburtstag Tikip santakki mala bashmu.. (Cuneiform Monographs). Groningen. Styx Publications. 1998
660-J.J.A. van Dijk. La Sagesse suméro-accadienne. Leiden. Brill. 1953
661-Le fête du nouval an dans un texte de Shulgi. Bibliotheca Orientalis 11. 1954
662-Une insurrection générale au pays de Larsha avant l'avènement de Nuradad. Journal of Cuneiform Studies 19. 1965
663-VAT 8382: Ein zweisprachiges Königsritual.Heidelberger Studien zum Alten Orient. Adam Falkenstein zum 17. 1966. Edzard, D.O., ed. Wiesbaden: Otto Harrassowitz. 1967
664-Nicht-kanonische Beschwörungen und sonstige literarische Texte. (Vorderasiatische Schriftdenkmäler der Staatlichen Museen zu Berlin Neue Folge, Heft I (Heft 17). Berlin: Akademie-Verlag. 1971

665-Incantations accompagnant la naissance de l'homme. Orientalia 44. 1975

666-Cuneiform texts of varying content. (Texts in the Iraq Museum 9). Leiden. Brill. 1976

667-Ishbi'erra, Kindattu, l'homme d'Elam, et la chute de la ville d'Ur. Journal of Cuneiform Studies 30. 1978

668-LUGAL UD ME-LÁM-bi NIR-GÁL. Le récit épique et didactique des Travaux de Ninurta, du Déluge et de la Nouvelle Création. 2 vols. Leiden. Brill. 1983

669-Le motif cosmique dans la pensée Sumérienne." Acta Orientalia 28. 1964-65

670-L'hymne à Marduk avec intercesson pour le roi Abi'eshuh. Mitteilungen des Instituts für Orientforschung 12. 1966-67

671-Vanstiphout, H.L.J. Lipit-Eshtar's Praise in the Edubba. Journal of Cuneiform Studies 30. 1978

672-How did they learn Sumerian?" Journal of Cuneiform Studies 31. 1979

673-An essay on The home of the fish. Studia Paulo Naster oblata. Quaegebeur, Jan, ed. (Orientalia Lovaniensia Analecta 13). Leuven: Departement Oriëntalistiek, Leuven / Uitgeverij Peeters. 1982

674-Lore, Learning and Levity in the Sumerian Disputations: A Matter of Form, or Substance. Dispute Poems and Dialogues in the Ancient and Medieval Near East. Reinink, G. and Vanstiphout, Herman L.J., eds. (Orientalia Lovaniensia Analecta 42). Leuven. Peeters. 1991

675-The Banquet Scene in the Sumerian Debate Poems. Res Orientales 4. 1992

676-The Mesopotamian Debate Poems. A General Presentation. Part II. The Subject. Acta Sumerologica 14. 1992

677-Repetition and Structure in the Aratta Cycle. Mesopotamian Epic Literature: Oral or Aural? Vogelzang, Marianna E. and Vanstiphout, Herman L.J., eds. Lewiston/Queenston/Lampeter. The Edwin Mellen Press, 1992.

678-Tha Matter of Aratta: An Overview. Orientalia Lovaniensia Periodica 26. 1995

679-Sumerian Canonical Compositions. C. Individual Focus. 5. Disputations: Canonical Compositions from the Biblical World. Hallo, William W., ed. Leiden. New Yor. Köln. Brill. 1997

680-Sumerian Canonical Compositions. C. Individual Focus. 6. School Dialogues. The Context of Scripture, I: Canonical Compositions from the Biblical World. Hallo, William W., ed. Leiden. New York. Köln. Brill. 1997

681-The man from Elam. A reconsideration of Ishbi-Erra Hymn B. Jaarbericht Ex Oriente Lux 31. 1989-90

682-Sanctus Lugalbanda. Thorkild Jacobsen Memorial Volume. Abusch, T. and Steinkeller.

683-Reflections on the dream of Lugalbanda: a typological and interpretative analysis of LH . Comptes Rendus des Rencontres Assyriologiques Internationales 43.

684-Vanstiphout, Herman L.J. and Alster, Bendt. Bird and Fish. A Sumerian Debate and Fable, or: The Importance of Being Pleasant. Groningen/Philadelphia/Copenhagen, 1988-96.

685-Veldhuis, Niek. Elementary Education at Nippur. The Lists of Trees and Wooden Objects. Groningen, 1997

686-The Sur$_9$-Priest, the Instrument gishAl-gar-sur$_9$, and the Forms and Uses of a Rare Sign." Archiv für Orientforschung 34-35. 1997-1998

687-Vincente, Claudine-Adrienne. "The Tall Leilan Recension of the Sumerian King List." Zeitschrift für Assyriologie 85. 1995

688-Volk, Konrad. Inanna und Shukaletuda. Zur historisch-politischen Literaturwerkes. (SANTAG 3). Wiesbaden: Harrassowitz Verlag, 1995

689-Waetzoldt, H. Review of Farber 1973. Bibliotheca Orientalis 32. 1975

690-Watson, W.G.E. "Review of Alster 1972." Scripture Bulletin 6. 1975

691-Die Sumerische Königliste und erzählte Vergangenheit. Vergangheit in mündlicher Überlieferung. Ungern-Sternberg, Jürgen von and Reinau, Hansjörg, eds. (Colloquium Rauricum 1). Stuttgart: B.G. Teubner. 1988

692-Genealogical and Geographical Thought in the Sumerian King List. DUMU-E$_2$-DUB-BA-A. Studies in Honor of Åke W. Sjöberg. Behrens, Hermann, Loding, Darlene and Roth, Martha

T., eds. (Occasional Publications of the Samuel Noah Kramer
Fund 11). Philadelphia University Museum. 1989
693-Die Emar-Version von "Dattelpalme und Tamariske" - ein
Rekonstruktionsversuch. Zeitschrift für Assyriologie 79 . 1989
694-Zu Gilgamesh und Akka. In dubsar anta-men: Studien zur
Altorientalistik: Festschrift für Willem H.Ph. Römer zur
Vollendung seines 70. Lebensjahres mit Beiträgen von Freunden,
Schülern und Kollegen. Dietrich, Manfried and Loretz, Oswald,
eds. Alter Orient und Altes Testament. Münster: Ugarit-Verlag,
1998
695-Review of Ferrara 1973. Die Welt des Orients 9 -1977-78
696-Lugalbanda in Reallexikon der Assyriologie. Edzard, Dietz
Otto, ed. 1987
697-Kollationen zu den sumerischen literarischen Texten aus
Nippur in der Hilprecht-Sammlung Jena. (Abhandlungen der
Sächsischen Akademie der Wissenschaften 65/4). Berlin.
698-Witzel, Maurus. "Die Klage über Ur." Orientalia 14. 1945
699-Wolkstein, D. and Kramer, Samuel Noah. Inanna, Queen of
Heaven and Earth. New York: Harper and Row, 1983
700-Wu, Yuhong. The earliest war for the water in
Mesopotamia: Gilgamesh and Agga. NABU.1998
701-Zgoll, Annette. Der Rechstfall der En-hedu-Ana im Lied nin-
me-shara. (Alter Orient Und Altes Testament 246). Münster.
Ugarit-Verlag, 1997
702-Zólyomi, Gábor. Speaking cow or mooing sorcerer? A note
on Enmerkar and Ensuhkeshdanna l. 173-4 (186-7). NABU.1995
703- Hugo Radau. Sumerian Hymns and Prayers to God Dumu-
zi or Babylonian Lenten Songs From the Library of Nippur.
Volume XXX. Munich. 1911
704-Stephen Herbert Langdon. The H. Weld-Blundel Collection
in the Ashmolean Museum. Volume One, Sumerian and Semitic
Religious and Historical Texts. Vol. 1.Oxford. 1923
705-H. Sayce. The Gods of Babylonia. The Hibbert Lectures on
the Origin and Growth of Religion as illustrated by the religion of
the Ancient Babylonians. Kessinger Publishers of Whitefish.
London & Oxford. 1897.
706-Nancy K. Sandars. Introduction to The Epic of Gilgamesh.
Harmondsworth, Middlesex. Penguin Books. 1960, 1969

707-Robert Graves and Raphael Patai. Hebrew Myths: The Book of Genesis. New York. Doubleday & Co. 1963, 1964. Greenwich House. Reprinted. 1983

708-Gwendolyn Leick. Sippar, a tale of two cities. Mesopotamia, the Invention of the City. Penguin Books. London. 2001, 2002

709-James Strong. Hebrew and Chaldee Dictionary. Word Books. Waco, Texas. 1977

710-Andrew George. The Epic of Gilgamesh, The Babylonian Epic Poem and Other Texts in Akkadian and Sumerian. Penguin Books. London. 1999

711-Victor P. Hamilton. The Book of Genesis. William B. Eerdmans. 1990

712-Arno Poebel and Sumerian Grammar. Samuel Noah Kramer. In the World of Sumer, An Autobiography. Detroit. Wayne State University Press.1986

713-A. R. Millard. The Etymology of Eden in <u>Vetus Testamentum</u>. Vol. 34.1984

714-William B. Eerdmans. In Eden. On the Reliability of the Old Testament. Publishing Company Grand Rapids. Michigan & Cambridge. 2003

715-Hugo Radau. Sumerian Hymns and Prayers to God Dumu-zi or Babylonian Lenten Songs From the Library of Nippur. Volume XXX. Rudolf Merkel of Erlangen Munich. 1911

716-John Ashton & Tom Whyte. The Quest For Paradise, Visions of Heaven and Eternity in the World's Myths and Religions. Harper. San Francisco. 2001

717-Jeremy Black, Graham Cunningham, Eleanor Robson & Gabor Zolyomi. The Literature of Ancient Sumer. Revised. Oxford University Press. New York & Oxford. 2004

718-Une Historie du Parais: Le Jardin des delices. Librarie Artheme Fayard. Paris. 1992

719-Joseph Blenkinsopp. The Pentateuch, An Introduction to the First Five Books of the Bible.. Doubleday. New York. 1992

720-Joseph Campbell. The Masks of God: Occidental Mythology. Viking Penguin Books. New York. 1964, 1991

721-Eric H. Cline. The Garden of Eden. From Eden to Exile. Unraveling Mysteries of the Bible.. National Geographic. Washington, D.C. 2007

722-Harriet Crawford. Pastoralists and farmers. Sumer and the Sumerians. Cambridge University Press. Cambridge. 1991, 2004
723-Jean Delumeau. History of Paradise: The Garden of Eden in Myth and Tradition. 1979
The Continuum Publishing Company. New York. 1995
724-Jack Finegan. Handbook of Biblical Chronology. Principles of Time Reckoning in the Ancient World and Problems of Chronology in the Bible. Peabody, Hendrickson Publishers. Princeton University Press. Massachusetts. Revised edition. 1998
725-Benjamin R. Foster. The Epic of Gilgamesh. W. W. Norton & Company. New York & London. Revised Edition. 2001
726-Tikva Frymer-Kensky. In the Wake of the Goddesses, Women, Culture and the Biblical Transformation of Pagan Myth. Ballantine Books. 1993
727-Andrew George. The Epic of Gilgamesh, The Babylonian Epic Poem and Other Texts in Akkadian and Sumerian. Penguin Books. London. Revised edition. 2003
728-Robert Graves & Raphael Patai. Hebrew Myths: The Book of Genesis. Doubleday & Company. New York. 1964
729-Victor P. Hamilton. The Book of Genesis. William B. Eerdmans. 1990
730-Alexander Heidel. A Special Usage of the Akkadian Term Sadu. The Journal of Near Eastern Studies. Vol. 8. No. 3. 1949
731-Morris Jastrow, Jr. The Religion of Babylonia and Assyria. Ginn & Company. Boston. 1898
732-Samuel Noah Kramer. The Babel of Tongues: A Sumerian Version. Eisenbrauns. Winona Lake, Indiana. 1994
733-Samuel Noah Kramer. The Sumerians, Their History, Culture, and Character. University of Chicago Press. Chicago. Rev. 1963
734-Stephen Herbert Langdon. Sumerian and Semitic Religious and Historical Texts. The H. Weld-Blundel Collection in the Ashmolean Museum. Volume One. Oxford. 1923
735-David Leeming. Jealous Gods and Chosen People, the Mythology of the Middle East, A new perspective on the ancient myths of modern-day Iraq, Turkey, Egypt, Syria, Lebanon, Israel,

Palestine, Jordan, Yemen, the Gulf States, and Saudi Arabia..
Oxford University Press. New York. 2004
736-Jean Delumeau. History of Paradise: The Garden of Eden in
Myth and Tradition.
The Continuum Publishing Company. New York. 1995
737-Jack Finegan. Handbook of Biblical Chronology. Principles
of Time Reckoning in the Ancient World and Problems of
Chronology in the Bible. Peabody, Hendrickson Publishers.
Princeton University Press. Massachusetts. Revised edition. 1998
738-Benjamin R. Foster. The Epic of Gilgamesh.. W. W. Norton
& Company. New York & London. Revised Edition. 2001
739-Tikva Frymer-Kensky. In the Wake of the Goddesses,
Women, Culture and the Biblical Transformation of Pagan Myth.
Ballantine Books. 1993
740-Andrew George. The Epic of Gilgamesh, The Babylonian
Epic Poem and Other Texts in Akkadian and Sumerian. Penguin
Books. London. Revised edition. 2003
741-Robert Graves & Raphael Patai. Hebrew Myths: The Book of
Genesis. Doubleday & Company. New York. 1964
742-Victor P. Hamilton. The Book of Genesis. William B.
Eerdmans. 1990
743-Alexander Heidel. A Special Usage of the Akkadian Term
Sadu. The Journal of Near Eastern Studies. Vol. 8. No. 3. 1949
744-Morris Jastrow, Jr. The Religion of Babylonia and Assyria.
Ginn & Company. Boston. 1898
745-Samuel Noah Kramer. The Babel of Tongues: A Sumerian
Version. Eisenbrauns. Winona Lake, Indiana. 1994.
746-Samuel Noah Kramer. The Sumerians, Their History,
Culture, and Character. University of Chicago Press. Chicago.
Rev. 1963
747-Stephen Herbert Langdon. Sumerian and Semitic Religious
and Historical Texts. The H. Weld-Blundel Collection in the
Ashmolean Museum. Volume One. Oxford. 1923
748-David Leeming. Jealous Gods and Chosen People, the
Mythology of the Middle East, A new perspective on the ancient
myths of modern-day Iraq, Turkey, Egypt, Syria, Lebanon, Israel,
Palestine, Jordan, Yemen, the Gulf States, and Saudi Arabia..
Oxford University Press. New York. 2004

749-Gwendolyn Leick. Inanna and Utu. A Dictionary of Ancient Near Eastern Mythology. London. Routledge. Rev. 1991
750-Gwendolyn Leick. Sex and Eroticism in Mesopotamian Literature. Routledge. London & New York. 1994. Rev. 2003
751-Charles Keith Maisels. The Emergence of Civilization, From hunting and gathering to agriculture, cities, and the state in the Near East. Routledge London & New York. 1993
752-Patrick D. Miller, Jr. Eridu, Dunnu and Babel: A Study in Comparative Mythology. Eisenbrauns. Winona Lake, Indiana. 1994
753-Magnus Ottoson. Eden and the Land of Promise. Volume 40. Papers read at the Congress of the International Organization for the study of the Old Testament held August 24-29, 1986 at the Hebrew University of Jerusalem, Israel. Brill. 1988
754-James B. Pritchard. The Epic of Gilgamesh: The Ancient Near East, An Anthology of Texts and Pictures. Princeton University Press. Princeton. New Jersey. 1958.
755-Cyrus Gordon. Ugaritic Textbook, Analecta Orientallia. Pontifical Biblical Institute. Rome. 1965
756-John, Huehnergard, Ugaritic Vocabulary in Syllabic Transcription, Harvard Semitic Studies. Scholars Press. Atlanta. 1987
757-Jean Nougayrol. Textes Suméro-Accadiens des Archives et Bibliothèques Privées. (Ugaritica V, Mission de Ras Shamra). Geuthner. Paris. 2006
758-Harriet Crawford. Pastoralists and farmers. Sumer and the Sumerians. Cambridge University Press. Cambridge. 1991, 2004
759-James B Pritchard. Ancient Near Eastern Texts Relating to the Old Testament, Princeton University Press. Princeton. 1969
760-Louis Jacolliot. Occult Science in India and Among the Ancients. London: William Rider, 1919.
761-Ron Ormand, and Gill Ormond. Into the Strange Unknown. California Esoteric Foundation, Hollywood. 1959. Reprinted as Religious Mysteries of the Orient. A. S. Barnes. New York. 1976.
762-D. N Rawcliffe. Illusions and Delusions of the Supernatural and Occult. Dover Publications. New York. 1959

763-Charles Virolleaud. La légende phénicienne de Danel. Paris, Geuthner. 1936

764- S. H Hooke. Babylonian and Assyrian Religion, University of Oklahoma Press, Norman. Oklahoma. 1963

765-Wilson Kinnier. The Rebel Lands: An Investigation Into the Origins of Early Mesopotamian Mythology. Cambridge University Press. Cambridge. 1979.

766-Henrietta McCall. Mesopotamian Myths. University of Texas Press, Austin. 1990.

767-A. Leo Oppenheim. Ancient Mesopotamia: Portrait of a Dead Civilization. The University of Chicago Press. Chicago. 1977

768-The New American Bible. Catholic Book Publishing Co., New York. 1970

769-Richard Carlyon. A Guide to the Gods. New York. 1981

770-S. H Hooke. Middle Eastern Mythology, Penguin Books. New York. 1963

771- Gordon Stein. Encyclopedia of Hoaxes. Gale Research Detroit. 1993

772- Theodor H Gaster. The Canaanite Epic of Keret", JQR. 1974

773- Manfried Dietrich. Loretz, Oswald - Sanmartín, Joaquín, The Cuneiform Alphabetic Texts from Ugarit, Ras Ibn Hani and Other Places, Münster, Ugarit Verlag, 1995

774- Andrée Herdner. Corpus des tablettes en cunéiformes alphabétiques découvertes à Ras Shamra-Ugarit de 1929 à 1939 (Mission de Ras Shamra, 10), Paris, Geuthner, 1963

775- Cyrus H. Gordon. Ugaritic Textbook (Analecta Orientalia, 38), Roma, Pontificium Institutum Biblicum, 1965.

776- Charles Virolleaud. La Légende de Keret, roi des Sidoniens d'après une tablette de Ras Shamra, Paris, Geuthner. 1936

777- Emilio Villa. Le gesta di Karit-Naaman re di Tiro e di Sidone, SMSR. 1939

778- John Gray. The KRT Text in the Literature of Ras Shamra. A Social Myth of Ancient Canaan, Leiden, Brill, 1964

779- André Caquot, and Maurice Sznycer. Herdner, Andrée, Textes Ougaritiques. Tome I: Mythes et Légendes, Paris, Editions du Cerf, 1974

780- Anton Jirku. Kanaanäische Mythen und Epen aus Ras Schamra-Ugarit, Gütersloh, Mohn, 1962

149

781- Joseph Aistleitner. Die mythologischen und kultischen Texte aus Ras Schamra. Bibliotheca Orientalis Ungarica. Akadémiai Kiadò. Budapest.1959

782-Pelio Fronzaroli. Leggenda di Aqhat. Testo ugaritico, Firenze. 1955

783- Godfrey Rolles Driver. Canaanite Myths and Legends. Clark. Edinburgh. 1956

784- Gregorio Del Olmo Lete. Mitos y leyendas de Canaan segun la tradicion de Ugarit. Ediciones Cristianidad, Madrid. 1981

785-Rin, Svi - Rin, Shifa, 'Alîlôt ha-'elîm. Kol širôt 'ûgarît, Israel Society for Biblical Research, Jerusalem. 1968

786- Nicholas Wyatt. Religious Texts from Ugarit. The Words of Ilimilku and his Colleagues. Sheffield Academy Press. Sheffield 1998

787- Miklós Maróth. A Keret-eposz", Antik Tanulmániyok. 1969

788-Donald Boadribb, Tri Mitoj el Ugaritico: Baal kaj Anat-Krt-Aqht", Biblia Revuo 7. 1971

789- I. N. Vinnikov. Einige Bemerkungen zur Sprache der ugaritischen Keret-Erzälung", in Actes du XXV Congrès Internationale des Orientalistes, , Izdatel'stvo Vostocnoj Literaturi. Moskva (Moscow). 1962

790-Paolo Xella. Gli antenati di Dio. Divinità e miti della tradizione di Canaan, Essedue. Verona, 1982

791- Svi Rin. Acts of the Gods. The Ugaritic Epic Poetry., Inbal Publishers. Philadelphia. 1996

792- Umberto Cassuto. Biblical and Oriental Studies. The Magnes Press, Hebrew University, Jerusalem. 1975

793-Baruch Margalit. The Ugaritic Poem of AQHT. Text, translation, commentary, de Gruyter, Berlin. New York. 1989

794-K. T. Aitken. The Aqhat Narrative. A Study in the Narrative Structure and Composition of the Ugaritic Tale, Manchester University Press, Manchester. 1990

795- Godfrey Rolles Driver. Ugaritic and Hebrew Words. A. Schaefer, Geuthner. Paris. 1969

796- Klaas Spronk. The Legend of Kirtu. A Study of the Structure and Its Consequences for Interpretation. JSOT Press, Sheffield Academic Press. Sheffield. 1988

797-Mario Liverani. Storia di Ugarit nell'età degli archivi politici. Centro di Studi Semitici. Roma. 1962

798-Walter Röllig. Die ugaritische Literatur, in Altorientalischen Literaturen. Neues Handbuch der Literaturwissenschaft, Wiesbaden. 1978

799- John Gray. The Legacy of Canaan. The Ras Shamra Texts and Their Relevance to the Old Testament, Brill. Leiden. 1965

800-Mario Liverani. L'epica ugaritica nel suo contesto storico e letterario", in Atti del convegno internazionale sul tema: La poesia epica e la sua formazione. Accademia Nazionale dei Lincei, Roma 1970

801-Frank Moor Cross. Canaanite Myth and Hebrew Epic, Essays in the History of the Religion of Israel. Harvard University Press, Cambridge, Massachussetts. 1973

802- Paolo Xella. Ugarit et les Phéniciens. Idéntité culturelle et rapports historiques", in Ugarit. Ein ostmediterranes Kulturzentrum im Alten Orient. Ergebnisse und Perspektiven der Forschung. I: Ugarit und seine altorientalische Umwelt, Münster. Verlag. 1995

803-Jeremy Black, and Anthony Green. Gods, Demons, and Symbols of Ancient Mesopotamia. University of Texas, Press Black Austin, Texas. 2003

804-Graham Cunningham, Eleanor Robson, and Gábor Zólyomi. The Literature of Ancient Sumer. Oxford University. Oxford. Rev. 2004

805-Rainer M Boehmer. Die Entwicklung der Glyptik während der Akkad-zeit. Rev. de Gruyter. Berlin. 1965

806-Walter Burkert, Greek Religion. Harvard University. Cambridge. Massachusetts. 1985

807-Erich Ebeling and Bruno Meissner. Reallexikon. Reallexikon der Assyriologie. De Gruyter. Berlin/Leipzig. 1932

808-Thomas Bertram. Anthropological Observations in South Arabia. Royal Anthropological Institute of Great Britain and Ireland. 1932.

809-The Baladi curative system of Cairo, Egypt. Springer. Netherlands, 1988

151

810-Winifred S Blackman. The Fellahin of Upper Egypt, AUC. Cairo. 1927

811-Tewfik Canaan. The Decipherment of Arabic Talismans, Berytus. Beirut. 1937

812-Benz, Frank L., Personal Names in the Phoenician and Punic Inscriptions, Rev. Biblical Institute Press, Rome. 1972

813-Einar C. Erickson. Ishabah: Son of Abraham. Ancient documents confirm LDS Doctrine concerning the Magi. 2004

814-Ignace J Gelb. Computer-Aided analysis of Amorite, Anthropological Studies No. 21, The Oriental Institute of the University of Chicago, Illinois. 1980

815-W. F. Albright. The Archaeology of Palestine. Harmondsworth, Cambridge. 1991

816-Y. Aharoni. Archaeology of the land of Israel: from the prehistoric beginnings to the end of the First Temple period. Westminister Press, Philadelphia. 1982

817-Y. Aharoni. New Aspects of the Israelite Occupation in the North, Near Eastern Archaeology in the Twentieth Century, Essays in Honor of Nelson Gleuck. New York. 1970

818-A Ben-Tor, Archaeology of Ancient Israel. Yale University Press. New Haven. 1992

819-J.F. Brug. Literary and archaeological study of the Philistines. B.A.R. Oxford. 1985

820-Trude and M Dothan. People of the Sea: the Search for the Philistines. MacMillan New York. 1992

821-T. Dothan. Philistines and their material culture. Yale University Press, New Haven. 1982

822-R Drews. The End of the Bronze Age. Princeton University Press, Princeton. 1993

823-J.F. Drinkard. Benchmarks in time and culture: An introduction to the history and methodology of Syro-Palestinian archaeology. Scholars Press, Atlanta. 1988

824-Israel Finkelstein. The Archaeology of the Israelite Settlement. Jerusalem. 1988

825-I. Finkelstein and N. Na'aam. From Nomadism to Monarchy: Archaeological and historical aspects of early Israel. Biblical Archaeology Society. 1994

826-B. Halpern. The Emergence of Israel in Canaan Scholars Press, California. 1983

827-T. Levy.The Archaeology of Society in the Holy Land. Facts on File, Inc., New York. 1995

828-A. Kempinski. Rise of an urban culture: the urbanization of Palestine in the Early Bronze Age. Israel Ethnographic Society, Jerusalem. 1978.

829-K. Kenyon. Amorites and Canaanites. Oxford U.P. London. 1966

830-K. A. Kenyon. Archaeology in the Holy Land. E. Benn, London. 1979

831-H.D. Lance. The Old Testament and the Archaeologist. Fortress Press, Philadelphia. 1981

832-A. Mazar Archaeology of the Land of the Bible: 10,000&emdash. Doubleday, New York. 1990

833-M. Magnusson. Archaeology of the Bible. Simon & Schuster, New York. 1978

834-P.R.S Moorey. A Century of Biblical Archaeology. Cambridge, 1991

835-P.R.S Moorey. The Bible and Recent Archaeology. London. 1989

836-P.L. Niels. Canaanites and their land: The tradition of the Canaanites. JSOT Press, Sheffield. 1991

837-D. B. Reford. Egypt, Canaan and Israel in Ancient Times. Princeton University Press. Princeton. 1992

838-M. Roaf. Cultural Atlas of Ancient Mesopotamia and the Ancient Near East. Equinox, Oxford. 1990.

839-Ignace J Gelb. Computer-Aided analysis of Amorite, Anthropological Studies. Revised. The Oriental Institute of the University of Chicago, Illinois. 1980

840-David Mandel. Who's Who in Tanakh, Ariel Books, Tel Aviv, Israel, 2004

841-Sabatino Moscati. The Phoenicians, Abbeville Press, New Yo1k, 1988.

842-Joseph Martin Pagan. A Morphological and Lexical Study of Personal Names in the Ebla Texts, Missione Archaeologica Italian in Siria, University Degli Studi Di Roma, Revised. Roma. 1998

843-Babylonisch-Assyrische Lesestücke, Rylke Borger, Berlin, Rome, Biblical Institute Press, 1979

844--Die Personennamen den Keilschrifturkunden aus der Zeit der Konige von Ur and Nisin, Ranke, Leipzig, 1907

845--Neu-Babylonisches Namenbuch, Tallqvist, Helsingfors. Bonn, Vienna, 1905

846-Bibliographie Linguistique de L'Année 1997, Paris, 1997

847-David Marcus. A Manual of Babylonian Jewish Aramaic. University Press of America. 1981

848-Alger F. Johns. The Short Grammar of Biblical Aramaic., Berrien Springs. Andrews University Press. 1972

849-Targum Pseudo-Jonathan: Genesis. English translation of the Aramaic. by Michael Maher. Collegeville. Liturgical Press. 1992

850-Targum Pseudo-Neofiti I: Exodus. Translation by Martin McNamara. Collegeville: Liturgical Press. English translation of the Aramaic. 1994

851-John Bowker. The Targums & Rabbinic Literature: An Introduction to Jewish Interpretation of Scripture. (Genesis). Cambridge University Press, Cambridge. 1969

852-The Bible in Aramaic. Edited by Alexander Sperber. Leiden, Brill, 1959

853-Hebrew Aramaic English Dictionary. Complied by Marcus Jastrow. Shalom Publications. New York. 1967

854-Samuel A.B. Mercer, Assyrian Grammar with Chrestomathy and Glossary. Frederick Ungar Publishing, New York. 1961

855-Simo Parpola ed. Neo-Assyrian Dictionary, English Assyrian, Assyrians English. Mesopotamian Museum of Chicago, 2002

856-Samuel A.B. Mercer, Assyrian Grammar. London. 1921

857-Amélie Kuhrt, The Ancient Near East: c. 3000-330 BC Routlege, New York.1995

858-Stephen A Kaufman. Aramaic in the Anchor Bible Dictionary. Edited by D.N. Freedman. Doubleday, New York.1992

859-Joseph A Fitzmeyer. The Phases of the Aramaic Language, in A Wandering Aramean: Collected Aramaic Essays. Scholars Press. Missoula 1979

860-Klaus Beyer. The Aramaic Language, Its Distribution and Subdivisions. Vandenhoeck & Ruprecht. Göttingen..1986

861- Stephen A Kaufman, "The Pitfalls of Typology: On early History of the alphabet" 1986

862-Stephen A. Kaufman. Aramaic in The Semitic Languages. Edited by Robert Hetzron Routledge, New York, London. 1997

863-Stanislav Segert. Vowel Letters in Early Aramaic. 1978

864-D. Cohen. Neo-Aramaic. Encyclopaedia Judaica. 1971. J. N Epstein. A Grammar of Babylonian Aramaic. Jerusalem, Tel Aviv. 1960

865-I. Garbell. The Jewish Neo-Aramaic Dialect of Persian Azerbaijan. The Hague. 1965

866-J.C. Greenfield. 1995. Aramaic and the Jews. Studia Aramaica (JSS Supplement 4). Oxford. 1995

867-Y. Israeli. The Jewish Neo-Aramaic Language of Saqqiz (Southern Kurdistan). PhD Dissertation, The Hebrew University of Jerusalem. Israel, 1998

868-G. Goldenberg. Early Neo-Aramaic and Present-Day Dialectal Diversity. 2000

869-S. Hopkins. 1991. Review of Studies in Neo-Aramaic. W. Heinrichs (ed.). JAOS.1991

870-S. Hopkins. יהודי כורדיסתאן בארץ ישראל ולשונ The Jews of Kurdistan in Eretz Yisrael and Their Language. Pe'amim. 1993

871-Ezra Zion Melamed. Aramaic-Hebrew-English Dictionary. Feldheim. 2005

872-Andersen, F. I., and D. N. Freedman. The Orthography of the Aramaic Portion of the Tell Fekherye Bilingual. In Studies in Hebrew and Aramaic Orthography.

Edited by D. N. Freedman and others. Biblical and Judaic
Studies From the University of California, San Diego . Winona
Lake, Eisenbrauns. Indiana. 1992

***   ***   ***